D1288677

what college didn't teach you about getting hired

The Ultimate Guide to Finding the Right Job Fresh Out of College

jon nelsen

LifeLevelUpBooks.com

and other organizations may qualify for special terms when ordering quantities of this title.

For information, email info@jonnelsen.com

This book is printed in the United States of America.

Life Level Up

contents

introduction

You have brains in your head. You have feet in your shoes.
You can steer yourself any direction you choose.
~ Dr. Seuss

So before we dive into the meat of this book, let's talk about a few
fundamental principles that everyone on this planet can relate to.

These principles can not only shape the way you live your life, but
form the lens through which you view the world. I'm asking you to
read these and truly comprehend what they mean, because simply
grasping these concepts will be enough to change the trajectory of
your life and perhaps your family's life decades into the future.

And rather than hearing these thoughts from me (you don't know
me yet), I want you to hear it from people who have already made
their impact on the world. An impact that perhaps you might still
make as well…

YOUR MINDSET IS YOUR ONLY LIMITATION

I will not let anyone walk through my mind with their dirty feet.

~ Mahatma Gandhi

The snake which cannot cast its skin has to die. As well the minds which are prevented from changing their opinions; they cease to be mind.

~ Friedrich Nietzsche

Stop giving other people the power to control your happiness, your mind, and your life. If you don't take control of yourself and your own life, someone else is bound to try."

~ Roy T. Bennett, The Light in the Heart

LEARNING MASTERY HAS A METHOD

If people knew how hard I had to work to gain my mastery, it would not seem so wonderful at all.

~ Michelangelo Buonarroti

Leadership and learning are indispensable to each other.

~ John F. Kennedy

It took me a lifetime.

~ Pablo Picasso

THE BEST TIME TO MAKE A CHANGE IS RIGHT NOW

"Everyone thinks of changing the world, but no one thinks of changing himself."

~ Leo Tolstoy

"Yesterday I was clever, so I wanted to change the world. Today I am wise, so I am changing myself."

~ Rumi

"Discipline is the bridge between goals and accomplishment."

~ Jim Rohn

If I have one singular goal through writing, it is to change the way people view themselves in the world around them. With this goal in mind each book is broken into three simple parts:

The Mindset
The Method

The Implementation

I do this because we live in a world that wants to make you small and take away your control. We're surrounded by people who want to tell us we're limited in what we can do, believe, or achieve. The worst part is if you don't learn to rewire your thinking, you can start to believe the nonsense and negativity.

Through mastery of your mindset you can train your brain to become your biggest asset and strongest ally. When you take the time to learn the best methods for accomplishing something, you increase your ability to achieve it exponentially. And finally, when you have learned enough to get started, it's time to take action. Implement the knowledge you have gained and start. Just start, don't wait, don't allow doubt to creep in, like Nike says, Just Do It!

I write each book to help you fully understand the most basic ideas of a concept and remove the illusion that rapid change takes dramatic effort.

- Life is a series of small steps and tiny victories. Decide who you are, what you believe in, then test why you have those beliefs.
- Decide what your goal is and make sure it matters to you on a deeper level.
- Visualize your achievement of the goal
- Then work BACKWARDS from that goal to where you are today. Create the steps, think about the obstacles, and make them so small and manageable that each day, week and month you are continuously marching towards your dreams.

I have written several books and I hope that this will be a lifelong effort demystifying the anxieties, worries, and stresses people maintain. There is no giant mystery to what I do, and I am not some uniquely gifted writer or philosophical thinker. I simply study the best advice and information available about a subject and distill it down into actionable pieces. Helping people just like you achieve what they want out of life by using a logical, systematic, and repeatable approach.

The keyword is ACTIONABLE, because you must choose to take action or you will never become who you want to be. For years I had the biggest dreams and the shortest attention span. I would aspire to greatness, but get overwhelmed by the process. It took a rewiring of my mindset to determine that breaking a goal into almost microscopic parts and achieving daily victories makes it easier to triumph than fail.

Why this book matters?

This book is about setting up the foundation of the rest of your life. It's about making choices based on both logic and your heart to discover the best career and life path immediately after graduation. After that it will show you step by step just what you need to make your dreams a reality. You will learn exactly **What College Didn't Teach You About Getting Hired**! Best of all, you will learn the exact process countless others have used to find meaningful employment in a career that fulfills them!

If you are the type of person who truly cares about reaching your potential and becoming the hero of your own story, visit me at: jonnelsen.com

Simply by visiting you will gain access to FREE books designed to build you up and resources to help you achieve maximum results for your life.

Good luck on the journey,
   Jon Nelsen

whom this book is for?

This book is for both those in college and recent college graduates. Written to help save you years of struggle and hardship. This is for those of you who are still struggling to find your path and those who have had known their future career since they were five.

If you are in college or recently graduated, now is the time to take the steps to design the life you always dreamed of. Follow my lead and learn from my mistakes. I will save you a decade or more of hardship. I will help you maximize both your earnings and happiness for your entire lifetime.

The years after college are not throwaway years. These are the most important life-defining moments that you'll ever have. You can't waste a minute not following the right path. Let me show you the step-by-step plan for the career of your dreams.

Jon Nelsen

life after college

. . .

THOSE FIRST FEW years after college are full of joy, excitement, and struggle. Days and nights can feel like they last a lifetime, and looking back you'll realize they were gone in the blink of an eye. But it is those first few years after college that lay the foundation for your future and the rest of your life. The choices you make now in relationships, where you live and what you do will stick with you forever. If you are not intentional in your decisions, you might wake up one day and realize you're living as a passenger in your own life.

When I began college, I was anything but intentional. While I wish I could say that upon graduation that changed, it did not. I spent years of my 20s struggling. I hadn't yet clarified my goals and established the path to reach them. In fact, I was years away from even deciding what I wanted my future to look like. I hope to save you a lost decade like I had and pave the way for you to live a life of success and abundance. It's easy, but it takes a bit of upfront time and effort upfront to reap rewards for a lifetime.

I've developed a straightforward system to follow. It will transform the way you view your career and align it with the lifestyle you want to create for yourself. By the time you finish this book, you will know exactly what jobs you should look for. You will know how they fulfill goals and dreams you may not even know you have yet.

The information in this short book might be worth hundreds of thousands of dollars throughout your lifetime. This is the most comprehensive no fluff guide to finding a job after graduation ever written, and I hope it guides you to real lasting success.

the problems

. . .

YOU FINALLY DID IT! Now what? After all those tests, all that homework, all those parties and all those years you finally graduated! We're told graduation is the key to our future. We're told that graduation launches us to a better life with more money. I hope this doesn't come as a shock to you, but life is always different from what you expect. We've seen our parents' struggle. We know family members who aren't making enough money. We have had friends that lived on the wrong side of the railroad tracks, living the life nobody wanted. They told us that if we work hard doors will open, so we worked as hard as we could. I'll let you in on a little secret. No matter who you are, finding a job sucks. That's because doors don't magically open up. A college degree does not always help and some might resent you for it. Those older generations that worked their way up through years of hard work are not happy about it. But don't worry, there's hope. I will show you the golden goose. I'm opening the doors to the kingdom. I will give you the answers to the test. Are you ready?

Imagine this! You sell everything you can, pack up the rest, and drive all the way from frigid Vancouver, Canada to beautiful sunny

Los Angeles, California. And not just some random place in Los Angeles. I'm talking about Hollywood! The gateway to the stars! You arrive and find out that having a place to sleep is more expensive than you thought. You end up in a hotel that's a little seedier than what you hoped it would be. That's okay. Everything is up from here. The world is your oyster and you will take what you can in this life. You go to bed with a smile on your face, knowing that tomorrow opportunities will come your way. Tomorrow you show the world what you're made of.

A brand-new job is around the corner. You'll have the shot of making more money than you ever dreamed of because you deserve it. You open your eyes, take a long relaxing shower, and shave to make sure you look as good as you can and put on your best clothes. You're prepared to hit the road to secure some interviews to begin the next part of your life. There's one problem, someone stole your jeep. You're in a new city, with no friends or family, without a job, and now without a car. What do you do? Do you know the saying "When life gives you lemons, make lemonade"? Ryan Reynolds squeezed the heck out of those lemons to make his lemonade. That's what happened on the famous actor's first day in Hollywood. So remember, as you're going through this annoying process, it could always be worse.

What a terrible example. A broke and jobless Ryan Reynolds taking the bus still has more going for himself than I ever will. I mean, look at that million-dollar smile! But I bet you have more going for you than you think. You willing to work and work to achieve your dreams right? You were told to find a job you love that pays you what you deserve, which would open the door to the rest of your life right? Guess what, your generation has received a check you can't cash. They said a degree and hard work is all you need to get you where you want to be in life. While that may have been the case a generation ago, that's not the case anymore. A degree now assures you of only one thing. That you'll spend the next 10 to 15 years of your life (if you're lucky) paying off that student loan bill. It is not their fault and you shouldn't be mad at them because it's what they were told and it's what they mistake for solid advice. It's the people that run colleges, text book publishers, and the hiring companies that want you to be desperate for money that are pushing for this agenda. These are the three major problems are crippling first time entrants into the job market. These problems apply to everyone. They are universal, and they can set you back decades if you make the wrong choice and don't overcome them. These problems will overcome most people and they will accept defeat, but you are not most people. Not only are we going to discuss the problems, but we will also turn them into opportunities. While everyone else is falling behind, you can get ahead of everyone around you and lap all your peers.

Problem 1: LACK OF EXPERIENCE AND COMPETITION

There's no getting around this one, it's a doozy. Look at most job postings. They want three years of experience and a degree for a job that pays $3 bucks over minimum wage. Yep, that will not cut it, but what can you do? Whether you like it or not, work experience is critical to snagging the job, and it makes sense. Let me tell you why.

One of the largest expenses a company has is the training and development of its employees. Companies are constantly developing and training their workers' for additional responsibility within the organization. Along the way they incur a major cost of money, time, and resources invested into this person. Unfortunately, the younger you are, the less likely the company will see their investment dollars returned. So putting it bluntly, they're no longer interested in investing in you. "A recent Gallup report on the millennial generation reveals that 21% of millennials say they've changed jobs within the past year, which is over three times the number of non-millennials who report the same. Gallup estimates that millennial turnover costs the U.S. economy $30.5 billion annually."[1]

Ouch, these companies have a point. A surefire way to put yourself out of business is to hire a bunch of millennials. You train them to do the work that you need them to do. Then they will ghost you for your competitor that can pay them $3 an hour more because they didn't have to spend a nickel to train them in the first place. That is a problem for both companies and the upcoming generation of aspiring workers. Those sobering statistics will incentivize no one to invest cash, time, or training into your future. So in order to get ahead in this world, you will need to make that investment yourself. You need to find the time, to get the training, to make the money. And you need to do it fast!

Over half of the graduate recruiters that took part in a recent research study by Highfliers said that "graduates who have had no previous work experience at all are unlikely to be successful during the selection process and have little or no chance of receiving a job offer for their organizations' graduate programs." [2]

In the past and much like today, traditional entry-level jobs did not always pay that much. But these jobs give you exposure to the field you were interested in, thus giving you experience. The trade-off was not getting paid as much as you'd like because the company was also dealing with the added investment in your training. Once you succeeded in that role, you would move up the company into better and better-paying jobs. In an ideal world, that would still be the case. Unfortunately, in today's interconnected modern economy, it is not. Somehow jobs that were once considered entry level now expect someone to have years of experience. That is because some pencil pushing nerd in a cubicle somewhere discovered that if they were slightly more selective in their hiring process, the company could have their cake and eat it too! They could find someone to work for peanuts and pay them like a monkey, all without having to make the big dollar investment into their future. In an increasingly interconnected and competitive job market, it often just becomes a waiting game for employers to find desperate candidates willing to break their back and work for less than they are worth. I like to compare the current job market to tinder for employers. You might be the best-looking guy in your town, but there are 100 other towns with 100 other guys just a swipe away. So just like tinder, if you want that HR manager to swipe right, you really need to yourself stand out! I know that might sound discouraging now, but it's about to get a lot worse before it gets better. But stick with this book and by the end you will be the one with jobs fighting over you!

Your generation has more going against it than any generation in history. We now have what's considered a global economy. And while it's great that it allows us to get our phone made in China at a discount, it makes the job hunt that much more difficult. This global economy exposes companies to the many benefits of global hiring. And unfortunately, if a company is only looking at the dollars and cents of outsourcing jobs, it's a no brainer. With millions of workers around the globe qualified to do your job, there will always be someone somewhere willing to do it cheaper. Let me be clear about one thing. It's a losing battle for the local worker to compete against global workers. For a crystal clear example, watch American Factory, a Netflix documentary produced by former President Barack Obama and his wife, Michelle. It's the story of a successful Chinese windshield manufacturer that opened a manu-facturing plant in the US. It's worth watching. I won't spoil it for you. But there was one thing that I took from this that scared me more than anything. It's the fact that the Chinese workers in this documentary would work 12 hours a day, six or more days a week for less money. Not only that, but they considered themselves lucky for the opportunity. If you are a recent graduate, that's a terrifying realization to have. There are dozens of countries around the world where employees will work harder for less and are often more experienced in your field. Why would a business hire you when they can pay people who will work twice as hard for half as much? Are you worried for your future yet? Fear not, my friends, I will provide you the solutions to survive and thrive in this global economy.

Another area that is a ticking time bomb to your generation is automation. THE ROBOTS ARE COMING! No, that's not the name of the futuristic sci-fi thriller playing at your local cinema. That's the reality of the coming automation in almost every industry. If you're worried about a foreign worker doing your job for less money, then you should be terrified about a robot working for free. "Over the next decade, the U.S. is projected to lose more than 1.5 million jobs to automation. China is slated to lose almost 12.5 million, the European Union will lose nearly 2 million jobs and South Korea will lose almost 800,000. Other countries around the world are expected to lose 3 million jobs to robots by 2030."[3]

Most of this will come in the form of replacement of factory workers by robotics. But even if you are not in the manufacturing field, you will still feel the repercussions of automation. When someone's job is displaced, they often retrain for a new field of work — often a field less susceptible to automation replacement. Imagine you are a company hiring your next employee. Who are you more likely to hire, the recently laid off supervisor with a successful track record of overseeing projects and people or the recent graduate with no experience but a similar salary request? If you would hire the supervisor, you're right.

Have I made my point clear? Do you now see why experience is necessary? Why the global economy harms the graduates? And how the future increase in automation will be detrimental to your job prospects? Before we get to the solutions, it is important to go over a couple more obstacles between you and the job you enjoy.

Problem 2: YOU HAVE NO MONEY

Another major obstacle is the fact that you're likely not rolling in the dough. Of course I'm speaking in generalities since I have no idea what your financial situation is, honestly don't care. You could come from a wealthy family, and this section doesn't even apply to you. If that's the case, good for you skip this part. For everyone else, going to college means coming out of it with student loans. You also need to save up to buy a home (renting is a losing battle, but that's for another book). You also need a vehicle that's reliable enough so you can get to this job you're hoping to have. Here are some sobering statistics. According to Forbes, "The latest student loan debt statistics for 2020 show how serious the student loan debt crisis has become for borrowers across all demographics and age groups. There are 45 million borrowers who collectively owe nearly $1.6 trillion in student loan debt in the U.S. Student loan debt is now the second-highest consumer debt category - behind only mortgage debt - and higher than both credit cards and auto loans".[4]

Your parents could graduate from college with little debt by flipping burgers as their part-time job to pay for school. In your case, you would have to make the equivalent income that an entire household makes in a year. The average student loan debt is $37,172[5] and in some states, the average household income is only $44,097.[6] Facing that depressing figure, what is a recent graduate to do?

The other issue with not having enough money is that it often forces you to take the first decent job offer that presents itself. There's just one problem, we're not looking for a "decent" job — we're looking for a job we love. Taking a job that doesn't pay as much can also set you back up to a decade for future salary negotiations. "Your first 10 years in the labor market likely shape your lifetime earning potential."[7] So you must set yourself up with the job that will allow you to make money in this competitive future. A wrong decision in your first career could make a difference of hundreds of thousands of dollars over the course of a lifetime. Later in this book, I will dive into side hustles for those of you who want to make a little money on the side, but wouldn't consider it your career. And who knows sometimes those little side hustles turn into regular hustles and end up not only paying the bills, but being something we enjoy.

So I hope you understand how important this major decision is. Don't take it lightly and without preparation. It's not something you decide on the advice of your drinking buddies or old roommate.

Problem 3: YOU HAVE NO SKILLS

Finally, let's go to the last issue facing all recent graduates today. That's your skill set. The glorious thing about college is that it allows you to see a variety of new things. It often teaches you theories that relate to your career, but life is not always theories. Sometimes life and work differ completely from they prepared you for. When you graduate and enter the career that you trained for, you're met with surprises along the way. But why would there be surprises, you ask? Well, college takes years. During which, there can be huge advancements in your field. While your teacher is busy teaching you instead of working in the field, they're missing out on crucial industry changes. These are the changes that may leave you unprepared when you enter the workforce. Your skill set is defined by on-the-job experience. Even if you were lucky enough to score an internship in your field, you might not have gotten opportunities on the right projects. The right projects are the kind that give you growth, knowledge and increased understanding. The good thing is you may have done work in the past that translates to the work you hope to do. Did you work a part-time job that helped teach you leadership skills? There are ways to maximize the appearance of minor tasks to fit with what the hiring manager is looking for. There are also ways that you can explain those skills and look like an idiot who is trying to justify why their summer lifeguarding experience somehow equipped them to manage a bank branch. Things you've done in the past can always be an advantage and help you achieve your goals for the future. However, present those same experiences incorrectly and you can fail your interview before it even starts.

This book is one-of-a-kind and not only because I wrote it. When I graduated there was nothing like this. Nothing prepared me for what was ahead. Sure "how to get a job" books existed, but none that showed the nitty gritty. No books that gave me all the tips, tricks and life hacks needed to and why I needed them. If someone would have sat me down and slapped me in the face with the hard to swallow truth about how jobs work, perhaps that might have kicked my butt into gear. But probably it wouldn't have made a difference, and I would have gone right on wasting time with little regard for what was coming next. No one gave me the exact step-by-step method on how to get a job that set me up for the future, so we will never know. But you now have this book and thus you have no excuses if you look back in 10 years and are not where you set out to be when you started your career. You don't have to go through many of the pitfalls I experienced. With this book, you can speed up and reach your goal faster than those around you. I will teach you how to:

- Identify what your career should be and why

- Where you should live for the lifestyle you dream of and a career opportunities that would disappear

Jon Nelsen

- Provide the effortless steps to a perfect resume and cover letter that **WILL GET YOU NOTICED**

- Teach you how to nail an interview before it even starts

AND SO MUCH MORE...

THIS IS the only job book you ever need to read. Once you finish this, you'll be on the road to a career of your dreams. I'll even take the time to go over common mistakes that can set you back years in your career and how to avoid them. So if you're ready to grab life by the horns, take control of your future, and design the life and lifestyle that brings you happiness, joy, and money keep reading.

setting goals

. . .

LIKE ANYTHING IN LIFE, hard work makes the difference between success and failure. In this section, we will discuss your career goals and help establish your success. As author Lewis Carroll said in his book Alice in Wonderland, "If you don't know where you're going, any road will get you there." And that's the way life is. Unless you set a specific destination and work backwards, you will find it's often difficult to figure out the next steps to achieve your goals.

So the first step in deciding our goal is figuring out what success looks like to other people. I know what you're thinking, "I'm not the person who cares what other people think". That's fine. But in reality, life's a lot easier when other people see what you're working towards and support your decisions. So even if you are planning a life of marching to your own drum, you still need to establish what potential obstacles you might encounter. They can be your family, friends, or even your co-workers. After that decide how to deal with the upcoming obstacles, both foreseen and unforeseen. Sure, success looks different to everyone. But depending on your family and the friends that surround you, it may look one way rather than another.

For instance, money was never a big motivator in my family. My parents had the most respect for people that were helping others and creating a positive change in their communities. My father worked as a youth pastor in our church and my mother was a director at a retirement home. Both of them would put in long hours, but it wasn't for the money. What mattered to them was the difference they made in the lives of others. I'm not saying this to sound preachy (pun intended). What I want to convey is that if my goal in life was to get a job on Wall Street and make buckets of money, I might have faced resistance at home. Now my first job interest was that of a Wall Street investor. I'm not sure how many 8-year-olds dream of that, but count me among them. My parents always wanted the best for me. But I could never look to them as a sounding board for talking about that decision. Without their support and guidance, I found it difficult to know what steps to take next. My hope for this book is that I can help you have more freedom in your decisions. I also hope that you have a better understanding of what to expect from those closest to you when discussing your dreams and ambitions.

Your friends' and siblings' view of success can also be both a blessing and a curse. If your friends are money hungry, they may never understand why you'd want to get a job teaching kindergarten. And that situation works in reverse as well. So it's important to consider what success looks like to them. I hope you're in a situation where you have a wide variety of friends from different walks of life. That helps you for a variety of reasons, gives you a broader perspective and different opinions to draw on. We should never let other people stop us from doing what is best for our lives, especially our career. But it is important to consider their opinions, thoughts and ideas as well.

Often, those around us have a good idea of our skills and aptitudes. I have a good friend who believes he is a natural-born sales-person and could sell ice to an Eskimo. In reality, this friend is rather abrasive. He can usually start opinionated arguments that lead to resentment directed at him from anyone he meets. The key to being a good salesperson is being agreeable. A good salesperson should be able to form commonalities and bonds with customers. My friend lacks those skills. He spent years floundering from one unsuccessful sales job to another. This is because he was unwilling and unable to hear the advice given by those around him. So while it's important to not let people dictate what we do, it's also impor-tant to consider their opinions and valid advice. To be a wise, well-rounded person, listen to both positive and negative feedback. Then decide what you believe to be valid. Otherwise, you risk becoming someone who does not have the needed self-awareness to succeed. That can make your life more difficult than it needs to be.

Success According to Others

Your first assignment is to get a blank notebook and begin formulating your goals and plans. Hold onto this notebook as we will use it throughout this book and it will become invaluable to your job hunt. You will start by writing how you believe the people around you view success and how they might define it in your life. Start with your parents or whoever raised you and write their current careers. Then to the best of your ability, write three overar-ching values each one has. Then write five jobs you believe they would prefer for you to have. Repeat this assignment for your brothers and sisters, your five closest friends, and anyone else whose opinion matters to you. Again, if you only have three friends, that's fine. Use the three you have. The number isn't what's important. What matters is that you gather an idea of the opinions of everyone around you. Now once you have this information, you can do one of two things. You can keep it to yourself as your reference, or you can ask them to verify it and make any changes as they see fit. Make sure that the person you are sharing this with will not take offense to your guesses of their values and beliefs. If they will, it's best to keep this to yourself. If you decide to let them verify, make sure you explain to them you're working towards discovering a career path that might interest you. Someone might try to inject an opinion for what you should do rather than allow you to discover this on your own. Stay the course and remember this is your decision and no one else's. Take everything they say with a grain of salt. You are the one who has to live this life, so remember the only opinion that matters is yours! Unless you're married, in that case do what your wife says and save yourself some headache.

Your Definition of Success

The next step is deciding what success looks like to you. This is where you must decide what lifestyle you want to build for yourself. To do this, the easiest way is to take 10 minutes in a quiet space. Visualize what your life could look like in 5 years, 10 years, and 20 years. Picture the wife, picture the kids, and picture the white picket fence, if that's what you're all about. Or perhaps you're living alone traveling the country writing in your RV, that's fine too. Write whatever you picture in the next section of your notebook. Then write the part of that daydream that interests you most. Describe each as well as you can. Don't rush through this. It's critical to establish what kind of lifestyle you want to design for yourself. Notice I said lifestyle design because picking a career is more than just the job that pays you. It encompasses how we view our future and what matters to us. **Do this now**.

———

IT'S NOW time to discuss what makes you happy and what drives you. In your 5, 10 and 20-year daydream you need to write five motivators in your life. This could be money, power, respect, freedom, structure, making a difference, helping people, etc. The choice is up to you. Only you can answer this for yourself. Remember, we are talking about the way you will spend your time in the coming decades. So don't rush through this activity. What you pick should truly reflect things you value in life. Don't write the things that sound nice or you think you should put down. Pick the things that matter to you. If you don't care about helping people and you want to make loads of money that's okay write it down, this is your life. If you're looking to live a life in service to others but worry about how you pay the bills, save that worry for another section and write that motivation down.

When discussing what you want out of life, I think it's important to discuss Abraham Maslow and his Hierarchy of Needs. "This hierarchy ranges from more concrete needs such as food and water to abstract concepts such as self-fulfillment. According to Maslow, when a lower need is met, the next need on the hierarchy becomes our focus of attention."[8]

The five levels in his Hierarchy of Needs are:

Abraham Maslow developed his hierarchy of needs in 1943. Since then countless people have found happiness and fulfillment. The goal of all my books is to help you find fulfillment through your life. To help you reach a point of self-actualization and internal happiness. Employment is a low-level need in the safety category. This means it's necessary to figure this out before moving on to fulfill higher-level needs.

Right now you may ask yourself why the hierarchy of needs is important. The truth is that understanding it gives you a better idea on how you could live your best life. It explains why finding a good job that provides fulfillment is one part of your life. Finding a good job is foundational to the overall happiness of your life, because trust me when you hate where you work or can't find a job, it's difficult to be joyful and see the rainbows after the rain. And while a career that fulfills you is very important, your life's made up of many other parts that need attention too. So today, we'll be working to help meet our basic safety need for employment and security. Tomorrow we may work on becoming a better friend or family member, who knows? So keep this hierarchy of needs pyramid in the back of your mind, and take time to read other books of interest in this series. They will help you get closer and closer to fulfilling your need for self-actualization and genuine happiness.

What makes this book so special is that it will walk you through a simple, accurate method in finding a career. This book will help you build the foundation for a lifetime of success. In this next section, we will get to the meat of this subject. We will talk about some of the worst advice you will receive and why it can set your career back decades. These are innocent misconceptions that are often stated as facts from friends and family. You must see these coming and know how to react. After finishing this book you will know better than to follow unproven advice. I will also show you many paths to success. We will lay out an easy step-by-step method to get you where you need to go. It's easy, repeatable, and can work in almost any situation. What I'm about to ask you to do will take hard work and a bit of sacrifice. It will also take time, but anything of value in this life doesn't come easy. So if you're ready to take the actions now that will affect the rest of your life, follow me.

practical advice for the recent grad

. . .

THIS SECTION WILL BE a practical collection of methods to avoid the pitfalls of life for a recent graduate. I will tell you why some of the most well-reasoned advice is awful, and why common sense prevails. Your most powerful resource is your ability to reason and plan. For most of you, you're not tied down with a family and the primary person affected by your decisions is yourself. Nothing is holding you back from getting what you want! This is the best time to carve out your path and sprint towards your goals. Will you run around and chase after the wind? Or run this race called life with purpose?

I will begin this section by discussing a few things you may have already heard advice on. For now, I would ask that you throw any advice you heard into the garbage and start from a clean slate. Listen to what I'm about to tell you because it will form the foundation for your future and set you on the best footing for the journey ahead.

Grad School Is For Suckers

I got your attention with that one. I'm not saying grad school doesn't have its place for most people. It's just usually not the best use of your valuable time at this moment. There are only two specific reasons to go to grad school. If **you already know what career you want or someone will foot the bill.** Read that sentence again if you missed it, because those are the only reasons you should go to grad school right now. I'm not saying you should never consider it, and I'm not saying it doesn't have a purpose. Unless an entry-level position in the career you've chosen requires it, it's best to wait. Consider that as an option for the future. Even without grad school, you may already have enough student loan debt for a lifetime. Rather than citing different articles to back up my opinion, I would recommend you to go on Reddit. See what advice other people have gotten with grad school. More often than not, the advice is to wait, if not to forgo it completely.

Grad schools are an important tool in many careers since it may lead to an increase in earnings. Notice that I said 'may' because it does not always guarantee a raise as it once did. And unless someone else is footing the bill, the only certainty with going to grad school is that you've now increased your overall debt. Not to mention the time you need to work to pay off that debt. Another reason to forego this at the moment is that you may luck into a career that pays for it. Why pay for something today that someone else may pay for tomorrow? If you feel passionate about grad school, the best way to pursue it is to join industries where it's not required in entry-level positions but might be for future advancement. That way, if you prove yourself to be valuable to the company, they might pay for some or all of it. Worst-case scenario, you let your superiors know you are serious about your career and signal your willingness for advancement by getting a graduate degree. If you spend your time and money doing grad school right away, there is always a chance that you don't even enjoy the job you went to grad school for. You may find out that this dream career you always wanted is not anything like you envisioned once you enter the field. It's better to first transition into another similar career than loading up on unnecessary graduate school loans. Or, if you go to grad school, you may find it harder to leave your job. This is because of the added student loan obligations may limit your choices because of the financial implications of quitting. I consider grad school to be like wearing ankle weights to go surfing. Sure, once you hop on the board, it won't make much difference. But it sure as heck is a lot easier to tread water without them on your ankles.

Don't Limit Your Job Hunt to Only One Industry

In searching for a job, you need not limit yourself to only one industry. You need to prepare for many options rather than one. Post-graduation, your biggest goal should be to build your skill set. Find a job that offers a challenge, helps you learn, and grow. Make sure that job has transferable skills that others will value as much as you do. Your first job is also the basis for the rest of your earnings over your lifetime. It's what all future jobs will base salary negotiations on. That means it's important to make sure you're earning the most you can in your chosen field. As we job hunt, we will give more priority to jobs that offer increased pay and an ability to grow our skill set. That will provide leverage for your next job. If it provides transferable skill sets, you are also building your qualifications for the perfect job you may find down the road. It's important to be flexible, especially after graduation. You may believe you already know what you want to do, but until you do it, you don't really have a clue. But a similar job that has valuable transferable skills might be easier to gain at the present. You might even find that you enjoy that job, even though you never considered it in the past. Perhaps it could even become a fulfilling career one day. You will never know what you are potentially missing if you're close-minded and only interested in the industry that perfectly aligns with your degree.

Don't Give 100%

It's the first time you've ever heard this advice, isn't it? For your first post-graduation job, it's important to pace yourself out of the gate. You may believe giving it 110% as your pathway to success, and you're right. But in most cases, if you give a solid effort and keep yourself from getting overwhelmed, you'll last longer over the long term. Now I'm not saying become a slacker, but what I am saying is once you give 100% you have nowhere to go but down. When you're starting a new career, slow your pace down. Try focusing on doing things correctly and learning the proper procedures. Rather than giving everything you've got, focus on perfecting a few things at a time. Your employer would rather see that you're doing your job correctly than doing it fast. Doing one thing very well is always preferable to doing ten things sub par. Over the long term, it's easy to get overwhelmed if you overwork yourself. This is especially true when you're in an unfamiliar environment and you're coupling hard work with extensive training.

Forget Politics

Do you love to share your views and hear the opinions of others about how the world is and how it should be? College is often a time when professors spend great deals of energy looking to indoctrinate you with their beliefs. That's just fine and dandy if you wish to talk about that in the privacy of your home, but do you think you should be the person spouting off their beliefs to anyone who listens at work? If you do, you also may be the person who self-sabotages their budding career before it can even begin. Do not, and I repeat, do not engage in any political discussions at the

Jon Nelsen

workplace. Do not talk about politics with people you work with outside the workplace or on social media either. The thing about politics is that everyone thinks they're right. Everyone thinks the people opposite them are wrong. Often you'll sound like a smug idiot who believes you're somehow more knowledgeable than others. In the U.S., roughly 50% are Republicans and 50% are Democrats. Guess what? Even if you live in the most liberal cities, like Seattle or Portland, you may work with people who do not share your views. And people dislike feeling inferior because they believe something different.

When the discussion of politics comes up, it's best to say you're not interested. If you're pushed on the subject, you can explain like an educated individual you have complicated views. Tell them that there are certain areas that you feel more passionately about than others. You can also make it known that you don't buy into the beliefs of one system of thinking. People usually only care about a few core political values. They then adjust the rest of their core beliefs to fit the system that those beliefs best fall into. In that way of thinking, the only one you limit is yourself. No party is 100% right, and no party is 100% wrong. Like everything in life, it's good to find balance. So when you bring politics into work and make it your cornerstone, you might risk annoying someone who can help advance your career. Also, keep in mind that in college you're taught by professors that have a certain way of thinking. Yet, you may work in an industry or business that has a different way of thinking. This is an area where a little self-awareness goes a long way for your chance of future advancement.

Life Is Not Fair

Life isn't fair, and it never was. This should be something that everyone who graduates college should understand. But that's not always the case. That's why I have mentioned it often in this book.

You grew up in a country where you had the ability and means to go to college. You're also fortunate enough to be reading this book, filled with practical advice that some people may never get to hear. The advice in this book may be worth hundreds of thousands of dollars over the course of a lifetime. This is something that someone from a different country may never have the chance to see. Even without knowing you, I bet there are some areas in your life where you're blessed. That's nothing to feel ashamed of. In life, some people have and some people don't have. Both can lead to success or failure, and it's your mindset and discipline that determine what the future holds. Somewhere there's someone receiving an opportunity that you can never dream of. In the same way, somewhere there's someone whose dreams and hopes are being shattered. Life isn't fair, never was, and never will be. It's your job to do the best with what you're given for both yourself and for your family. If you hope to make life fair for others, doing that from a place of privilege and means is a more effective platform. So never feel ashamed that you have a good job or that you're making a decent salary. The world doesn't work like that. Just because you make more money, doesn't mean someone else makes less. In the same way, because you have the opportunity for a career that you enjoy and love, doesn't mean you're keeping that from someone else. Be thankful that even though life isn't fair, it still allows you to prosper and thrive.

Everything's Better with Money

As we have already discussed, I came from a household where the pursuit of money was not some glorious achievement. I didn't grow up lacking anything I needed, but sometimes more money would've made a major difference. If I have learned one thing is this, life is much easier with money. Even if your goal is to become a pastor like my father was, having money and resources allows you freedom in your decision-making. You don't have to worry about how you will pay for the next bill. You're able to make choices to benefit the long-term rather than the near term. Money could mean freedom. Freedom to decide who to help, what to pursue, where to live, and how much crap you take from a boss before you quit. When you're starting out, if all things are equal, go for the job that pays a little more. Then focus on using those skills you gain at that job to find your perfect career. Be able to negotiate your salary from a position of strength. Don't forget that the earnings during your first few years of employment will form the foundation for the earnings for the rest of your life.

a place to call home

. . .

WHAT DO I DO NOW?

By this point, we've learned about the problems that fresh grads face. These are the lack of experience, limited financial resources, and the lack of applicable job skills. We've discussed what success looks like to those closest to us and to ourselves. We've formed some goals and ideas about what we value in our careers. We have heard some practical advice that may run in the face of things we heard in the past. Now it's time to take the next steps. You'll learn a system for evaluating who you are, what you want to be, and how to become it. Let's get down to the nitty-gritty and answer a few of the most basic questions first.

Where Do You Want To Live?

Now the first major decision that will affect the rest of your life is deciding where to put down roots. While you could spend the first year or two after college traveling the world and that is your choice, you eventually need to settle on one location. Choosing the area you will live in is of the utmost importance and will affect most other aspects of your life. To some people it defines their level of happiness. When I was younger, I left my home state of Pennsylvania. I packed up my car and traveled across the country to California. This move allowed me to break out of my shell and experience the world differently. I lived a life that wouldn't have been possible back in PA. This move also set me back years in both my career and personal finances. Before I left, I had not spent the time to figure out what I needed to be happy in life. All I knew is that Los Angeles had palm trees, beautiful women, and miles upon miles of beaches. This, as I found out from experience, was not a recipe for success. Let me show you what I should've done.

Had I been a smarter, more industrious person like you are, I would've done the following:

• Decided how close I need to be to family and how often I will see them in the near and distant future
• Tested the job market
• Evaluated the economy of the state and its taxes
• Done a cost-of-living calculation between all the cities being considered
• Researched the cost of buying a new home
• Guesstimated how I could save money
• Decided if I wanted roommates again
• Figured out how I wish to spend my free time and what activities that location offers
• Weighed the quality of life that my choice would offer me

Let's go over each one and use it to inform how you will decide where you will live and why. Thinking about this decision helps you on many fronts. It's good to do basic research on what a location offers versus another. It helps you plan a goal. It gives you a physical destination of where you want to be. This can be powerful in helping you achieve your dreams. Because the more variables you remove from a decision, the more accurately that decision can be made.

How Close Do You Want To Be With Your Family & How Often Do You Want To See Them?

There is no getting around the fact that family matters. If you are not close with your family, or if your family is no longer in the picture, this is something you need not consider as much. But even in that case, it's important to decide how close you want to be to the place you once called home. First things first, you need to decide how often you'll see your family in the immediate future. Are you and your family close? Do you need to see your family on a weekly, monthly, or yearly basis? If you need to see your family weekly, don't live further than about one or two hours away by driving distance. If you're satisfied seeing them monthly, you could stretch that distance out to as far as five hours. And if you only need to see your family yearly, you could live about anywhere. But it will make the most sense to at least live on the same continent.

A weekly 2-hour round trip car ride for most people is not something that will be detrimental to their quality of living. That's the reason I chose those numbers. Remember, Maslow's Hierarchy of Needs is about maximizing your quality of life in fulfilling your needs. A relationship with family is a need for most people. When you stretch it out to a monthly visit, a ten-hour round trip each month would be a reasonable amount of time, though not as inconsequential as something shorter. You can still live at a distance while seeing your family enough to keep you happy.

It's also important to remember that your family can come visit you too. It doesn't always have to be you traveling to see them. However, you may wish to travel to see them more often if that's where your childhood friends still live. If you will travel to see your family any more than an hour or two, you need to at least have the

29

option of a couch to crash on when you visit. It would get expensive having to pay for a hotel every time you wanted to see your family.

Another scenario is that you may decide you want to leave home, but your family would let you move back after college. Doing this gives you freedom to establish your career and be more picky about what you choose. If this is the case, it might be your best option to set yourself up for success. That said, there are a few reasons it also might be a poor option.

Decide if you can live at home post-graduation and if you could deal with the consequences of that. Will you have the privacy you need to be happy and finally feel like an adult? Will you take this next stage of life seriously or will moving back into your old bedroom cause you to waste valuable time? If moving back home causes you to get back into the routines of someone who is not career oriented or trying to advance their life, that may not be the best idea even if rent is cheap or non-existent. Decide on what area you could picture yourself happy in. Then factor in the distance to your family. One thing I did not mention when making the evaluation are your friends, and that is because friends come and go. Right now you may be very close to your friends and they may end up being your friends for life. But in most cases, the friends you have now won't be the friends you'll always have. So while it's okay to consider them, don't let the distance between friends be a major factor in your plans. You'll be shocked at how many friendships change when people get married, have kids, or move away.

How's The Job Market?

What does the job market look like in the places you're looking to move to? Is the job market strong? Are salaries competitive because workers are tough to find? Or are there few job openings fought over by many candidates? You should know situations like that only give the companies the advantage when it comes time for salary negotiations. A simple Google search will give you a good idea what the job market may look like over the next few years. Factors like current unemployment in the city or population growth. You only need to concern yourself with what the job opportunities may be for the couple of years. This is important because your initial salary can set the floor for all future salaries to come. Then if the job opportunities in the area shrink, you already have a starting point for future negotiations. Your job is providing you income that you can count on if you need to search for something new. When testing the job market, it's good to seek friends or people in your network who may help you land that first job. There are many ways to do this. One of the easiest ways is to tell people what kind of career you're interested in and ask if they have any leads for you. It might surprise you how many people will help you and how they can make your path easier.

How's The State Economy and Taxes?

Now, this may not be one of the sexier points on the list, but it is important to think about it. Over a lifetime, the city you live in can affect your ability to save by thousands and thousands of dollars. Also, it's important to look at the economics of your state. What percentage of the states' revenue is spent on social programs? How many new businesses are entering the state and how many are exiting. For instance, a state like Texas has fewer public programs than California. That's often reflected in the amount of taxes its residents pay. Texas also is a lower cost alternative to California for businesses. That means the job market is growing and businesses have reason to expand operations. According to wallethub.com, "Taxpayers in the most tax-expensive states, for instance, pay three times more than those in the cheapest states".[9] So while you're young and you don't make as much, where you put down roots can have a big impact on your future cost of living. This brings me to my next point, which is the cost of living in your area.

How Does The Cost Of Living Compare With Other Cities?

Do you know how far your money goes? Before you ever discuss salary or going to your first job interview, you need to know how far your money goes. For instance, if you make $1000 a week in Oklahoma City and that same amount in New York City, your money will go a lot farther in Oklahoma. Cost-of-living will also be a factor during salary negotiations. So it's important to know how your region stacks up. You can Google the cost-of-living calculator. Type in all potential cities you are considering in your decision.

How Much Will A New House Cost?

This point is like the last one, but very relevant to new graduates. It is not advisable to buy a new home within the first year of your career. But more likely, it may be something you think about down the road. It's good to know how much it will cost to buy a home when the time comes. You should already know average housing expenses based on cost-of-living calculation. You might also want to look at the listings local realtors have in any areas you are considering.

Will You Be Able To Save Money?

Savings are key to your financial freedom and ability to live a life not always worrying about money. When making an evaluation of where to live, it's important to see how easy it will be for you to save money. Living at home may allow you to save more money for your future than living somewhere else. Yet, you may find that unbearable if your biggest goal is to have more freedom and get away from mom and dad. This point is simple. Look at all your available options. Do your best to decide which ones will allow you to save the most money and which will allow you to save the least.

Can You Live With Roommates Again?

Now that college is over, can you handle life with roommates again? If so, living with roommates for a few years while you're single is a great way to save money. If you're able to find a good roommate, it also can become a way to have a friend in a place where you may know no one else. So take a moment to decide if you can handle living with a roommate again, or if you need your own space. Always weigh the pros and cons of each. If you choose the roommate route, I would recommend that you first reach out on social media to friends and family. Check if they know of anyone searching for a roommate in the city you want to live in. If that doesn't work, it may be worth it to see the alumni network that your school has. Ask if they offer any resources to help you find someone. At the very least, you would have one thing in common. Then use common sense and good judgement. Ask lots of questions. Use web searches and social media to vet any potential roommates. Make sure you would feel safe with that person. It's also good to establish how much they may or may not want to hang out with you to avoid any miscommunication.

How Do You Want To Spend Your Free Time?

Let's say you can live near a free public beach and get to take advantage of a cheap way to spend an afternoon. Or perhaps you'll end up living near a world-famous golf course and want to take advantage of hitting those famous links. There's no right or wrong answer, only information for you to gauge your decision by.

Places with free natural resources where you could hike or swim offer more variety than a local dive bar. Remember, if drinking is your thing that's okay, but that's something you can find in most places. What you can't find everywhere are free activities in nature. So decide on what's important to you and how you wish to spend your free time. It should be one of your bigger considerations in picking a location to live in. What you do during your free time can end up costing you considerable money so factor that in your decisions.

Will You Have A Good Quality Of Life In That City?

Often, people confuse the cost of living with quality of life. They are very different and are looking at different metrics. Quality of life is adding up all the pros and dividing them by all the cons in calculating how happy you could be. Add considerations we've discussed and any we haven't. Weigh them against any negatives you revealed during your search. Quality of life is the most important thing an area can offer you. For instance, while living in Los Angeles, I experienced grocery store valet service. That was not something I had experienced in Pennsylvania. Not being able to park at a grocery store and then having to pay for that privilege detracted from my quality of life, even if only in a small way. So take some time and deep dive into the pros and cons of the cities you're thinking of. Try to calculate what your quality of life would look like if you lived there. When comparing multiple locations you can even take the list we discussed and give everything a number rating. Make sure you keep your metrics and reasoning consistent and objective. Then you can decide based on logic and data instead of just a feeling.

Through this exercise, I hope you had a lot of time to think about what's important to you. Deciding the place you will call home and where you will live is one of the most important choices, you may ever have to make. Because once made, it's difficult to fix if you mess up. So my advice is to go slow when making your considerations and take your time. Make sure you visit any cities and neighborhoods you're interested in both during the day and at night before ever deciding where you want to call home. Some cities look great during the daytime and are very different at night. So no matter where you pick to live, make sure you pick somewhere you feel safe. Moving somewhere where you don't feel safe detracts a lot from your overall quality of life.

what types of jobs can you find?

. . .

THIS IS AN INTERESTING QUESTION; what types of jobs are available? You are free to pursue any career in any industry that you find interesting. But your degree may have better prepared you for certain endeavors. We will now discuss both how to use your degree to find a job in your industry and how to leverage your degree to find a job in an unrelated industry. At this point in the book, you should have a basic idea of the area you want to live in. If not, make sure you continue to narrow down your search so you can begin the next step of researching jobs.

I Want to Work in a Field Related to My Degree

This first section is for people who like their degree and hope to work in a related field. I know not everybody fits into this category, so hang on and we will get to that next. It's important to begin this with an open mind so you don't limit yourself or your options. I will go over each step so you do it exactly right. Don't skip this part. Take your time when you do this. Remember, it's your future at stake.

Step 1 and 2: Search Jobs and Make a List

Do a Google search and look for jobs applicable to your degree. Spend the time to at least go through a dozen different websites and make a list. Not all degrees are equal and not all degrees offer the same job opportunities. When you finish you should have at least 30 degree specific jobs to choose from. You should then search for jobs that can be done with any degree and add everything that you find to your list. The goal here is to make the longest list you can and narrow it down later.

Step 3: Create A Spreadsheet With The Following Columns:

1. Job
2. Average Salary
3. Work-Life Balance
4. Room for Growth & Advancement
5. Passion and Excitement
6. Total Score

Take a moment to color-coordinate this. Make it look clean and attractive since you will spend a good amount of time looking at this. It should go without saying that you should save this often so you don't lose any of your work.

Step 4: Rank Each Job From 1 To 10 (1 As The Bad/Low And 10 As The Good/High) In Columns 2 - 5 And Then Add The Total Score In Column 6.

JOB	AVERAGE SALARY	WORK/LIFE BALANCE	ROOM FOR GROWTH	PASSION & EXCITEMENT	TOTAL
JOURNALIST	7	5	4	8	24
EDITOR	6	4	7	4	21
ETC					

ONCE YOU RATE EACH COLUMN YOU WILL THEN
PUT THEM IN ORDER FROM HIGHEST TO LOWEST
TOTAL SCORE

It's important to take your time here and get it right. Make an exhaustive list of all the jobs you found in the left column. List even the ones you're pretty sure you're not interested in. They will be wonderful comparison piece for the rest.

Average Salary

DETERMINE your criteria for each salary. Associate one through ten as a fixed number range. For instance, a seven might be anywhere between $45,000 and $50,000 annually. Your degree will determine your salary, but try to set five as the middle range between all available jobs on your list.

Work/Life Balance

The expected work-life balance won't be as specific as your salary. Setting five as your middle range should be able to put the lower and higher numbers in perspective. Here you are deciding if this is a job where 40 hours is the norm or exception. Is this a career where you will work on holidays or weekends and if so, how do you feel about that? No matter how much you might enjoy working all the time, it's important to consider that you have a life outside of work and will one day have a family that wants to spend time with you. If you already have this family, I'm sure you realize how important finding a healthy balance is. For this I would rank a 40 hour weekly job a high as that's a basic standard set of hours. Be sure to factor in if a job has lots of flexibility like that of say a Realtor. If a job will allow you to adjust your hours as life dictates that might be a high score. In the same way, if a job is a strict 9-5, and that's what you like, that would also be a high score.

Room for Growth

When trying to decide the expected room for growth and advancement, you must do some research in each field and draw conclusions. You may also want to consider if a job type is a good springboard for advancement into another field and factor that into the rating.

Passion & Excitement

For the next column, rate it according to how it excites you! Are you going to be jumping out of bed ready to get to the office, or do you think you will you dread the daily grind a week into your career? This is something only you can answer, and this will be rather subjective. Only you can decide if it's a job you have a passion for and that you can see yourself doing long term. Try to be as objective and realistic in this rating as possible. Don't be overly optimistic when rating, be honest. If you are a person who hates waking up each day, a job that begins at the crack of dawn might make you miserable.

Total

Add together average salary, work/life balance, room for growth, passion and excitement to get the total number in the last column and repeat this for each job on the list.

Step 5: Narrow Down Your List to the Top 20 Jobs

This part is straightforward. Sort that last column with the total scores from highest to lowest. Create a second spreadsheet with your top 20 choices on it. In the event there are some more jobs that you're interested in, add them after your top 20. You should have a good reason for choosing something with a lower score. So now you have a long spreadsheet that you can refer to after a few years. See if you still feel as strongly about your rankings after you have a bit of experience under your belt. By that time, you will have a more condensed spreadsheet of the jobs that are most likely the best fit for you.

I Picked a Stupid Degree that I Hate and Never Want to Work in that Field Again

This is for the people who aren't that excited about their degree choice and just finished it to get that slip of paper. Because of that, you have to do more legwork to find the golden ticket to the job of your dreams. This doesn't mean that it's impossible to find a job you love. It just might take you longer and will be more difficult. You will do everything from the last section, the same as those people who love their degree. But you will also do it using the ideal degree that you should have gotten. So you will need to decide what degree you would've picked in a perfect world. Make a job list for both the hypothetical degree and the degree that you actually did complete. You will then create a third spreadsheet with the top

20 jobs for both degrees. This third spreadsheet should have 40 top job choices and you will now also add any degree specific jobs that somehow appeared on both lists. That will give you a top jobs list of at least 40+ jobs to choose from. You will then have to use your best judgment to narrow them down to 20 so you can make a more accurate decision. A job that appeared on both lists might be your key to one day doing a job your degree doesn't deem you suited for. If you can take the degree you currently have, use it to find a job on the list of jobs your ideal degree is suited for, one day you could make the jump to a job of your choice on either list. Therefore, it's worth adding those extra jobs to your top 40 list.

I Double Majored, Does That Mean I Need to Do Two Lists?

Yes, you do. You will make two spreadsheet lists figuring out the top 20 jobs on each and then do a web search for jobs that use both degrees and add those jobs to the third spreadsheet list. You will have 40+ entries. I would pay special attention to jobs that both your degrees work towards because you may find quicker advancement because of that. You will then use your best judgment to narrow that list down to 20. Remember that the ones with the highest number may not always be the best for you, but have a good reason for discounting them.

Time to Narrow Down Even Further

I bet you thought the hard part was over! Not yet, but we are getting close to discovering your options in a logical and systematic way. Now that you've come this far, know where you want to live, and have a list of 20 top career choices, we will narrow your search further. The next part is to get down to five careers you want to search and apply for. Let's go over how to do that. Don't get sick of spreadsheets yet, because we're not finished. We still need to finish working on the one we already created. We are going to take that spreadsheet with the narrowed down list of 20 jobs and add the following columns to it:

1. Entry Level or Realistic
2. Number of Openings
3. Motivator 1
4. Motivator 2
5. Motivator 3
6. Motivator 4
7. Motivator 5
8. 5-Year Vision

Let me show you what all those columns mean and how they will help you narrow down your search to the five ideal career choices.

Entry Level or Realistic

In this column, it'll be a simple yes or no. Is this an entry-level job? Or is it a job you need years of experience in before becoming a realistic candidate? I added realistic because sometimes you have some outside resource that could help you skip an entry-level job. This could be a friend, family member, or contact that could help you get an interview for a job that you might otherwise not even be that qualified for. If that's the case, by all means, explore that opportunity. In fact, if you have a resource like that, be sure you add that one to the list if it's not already on your top 20.

Number of Openings

For this one, you will find the number of job openings available in the area you will work in. To do this, search five different job search engines. Use all the different combinations of what a hiring manager might call that job in your search. Limit your search to 30 miles or fewer from where you wish to live. On each of the five search engines, write the total number of job openings available. Add them all together and divide by five to find your average number of job openings to fill in this answer.

Motivators 1 - 5

Now is the time to revisit the five motivators you wrote in earlier in this book. In each of the next five columns, write the motivator you picked as the name at the top of the column. Then use your 1 to 10 ranking to decide how the job fits your motivator to the best of your ability. I know this will be difficult. It will take a good amount of guessing and thinking for each answer, but it's important to try your best.

5-Year Vision

In that same section, from part one, we discussed daydreams. We broke each into a 5-year, 10-year, and 20-year timeline. For this initial job search, we're only focusing on that five-year vision of the future. Now is the moment you need to reflect. Think about if this potential job would fit into that five-year vision you created. Could you see yourself in that career in 5 years and if so, would you be happy? You then use that 1 to 10 score to determine how close this job comes to hitting the mark of that vision.

Narrow the Field

So, by now, you filled in all the extra columns for each of the 20 jobs on your list. Any job on that list that is not entry level or realistic is out. That's not to say you can never revisit it, but for now, they are a no go. You will then have to use your data in the columns to take the remaining jobs and reduce them down to five. To do this, use the combination of data and gut feeling to come to your conclusions. Rank each of these remaining jobs in order from best to worst for you and those top five are now the ones you will apply to. Be sure to save this list, especially in a tough job market. This way, you can apply to jobs outside of the top five, yet inside the top 20 should you ever need to. You now have something that almost no one else has. You have a clear, reasoned and well-researched list of the best jobs for yourself. You can always revisit any of these lists when considering a career change. This can give you an idea of what to expect. This is one of the most valuable tools for your job searches. This list could be worth tens of thousands of dollars depending on how you use it.

preparing for the job

. . .

SO YOU NOW HAVE THE location you want to live and the top five careers you will pursue. Pat yourself on the back. You already have more clarification for your future than most people achieve in a lifetime. The best part is that none of this is a hunch or a guess. It's a well-researched plan designed to help you achieve the goals you set for yourself. Goals you established based on your own personal motivations. This is an incredible place for you to be. Now here comes the simple part, putting it all together and getting the job you deserve.

It All Starts with a Killer Resume and Cover Letter

Now is the part where you can shine. I will tell you the tips and tricks that will allow your resume and cover letter to shine. If you follow this, you will have a more professional and polished resume than most people twice your age. How does that sound? How does it feel knowing that when finished, the only thing standing between you and a dream job is an interview? I will teach you how to ace the job interview in the next section. For now, let's get started on the resume.

Step 1: Make A Word Document And List All Of Jobs You Have Had And Provide The Following Information:

• Name, address, and phone number of job

• Immediate supervisor or a supervisor you were closest to if they would give you a better reference

• Dates you worked there (month and year only) if they ask for a specific day on an application you can always say the 1st

• Tasks you completed at this job (list everything)

• Achievements no matter how small—this could be projects you finished that the boss liked, awards you received, or a measurable that helped the company either monetarily or through an elevated status

• Examples of Achievements - try to use numbers and stats to back up any achievements you state

• Any positive praise you have received from managers or owners (list their names and specific details about this encounter)

• Professional and personal references, their addresses, their phone numbers (be sure to ask anyone on this list ahead of time if you can use them as a reference)

• Past volunteering or clubs you took part in. If this is lacking, start volunteering immediately. That way you can reference it during upcoming interviews.

• Any certifications that you have received related to job skills necessary in your field.

Step 2: Visit Fiverr.com to Hire a Professional Resume Designer

This part is straightforward and for the lazy people reading this book. Visit Fiverr.com and hire a professional resume designer. Fiverr.com is an Amazon-owned company that allows you to hire people to help you with digital tasks. Type in resume on Fiverr and search through the services available. Visit each service provider's job posting. Make sure they have lots of reviews and examples of their resume designs. Most charge between $20 and $300 for resume services. I would find someone from your country to avoid any miscommunications. You will not need a high-end and expensive service at this point in your budding career. Hire the best one you can afford and provide them with the Word doc you created in step 1. Let them know the 5 types of jobs you will apply to with this resume so they can tailor it to the specific job. If the jobs you are looking for differ, it may be worth it to hire a second or even a third resume designer. The goal here is to have a resume that is industry specific for each job you apply to.

Look through the resume for any typos or false statements. Make sure it sounds professional and that the resume creator took what you did in the past and made it relevant to the jobs you are applying for. Ask some friends and family members to look this over, if they are in your prospective industry or have a high-level career that's even better. Get feedback and make adjustments as needed.

Another and better strategy is to learn to make a resume on your own using a template. I like to use canva.com which offers free accounts for light graphic design work. Type in resume and it will show you hundreds of templates. You would then do a web search for examples of resumes in your industry and try to match its tone and style. Never lie on your resume, but only include things that will put you in a good light. No need to include anything that doesn't help your cause, this includes past jobs.

The trick is to phrase everything the right way! Let's say you worked at a clothing store in high school, here is what not to put:

· · ·

- COUNTED DOWN the cash drawer to $300 each night
  - Answered questions from new employees
  - Made sure the customer was happy
  - Stayed late once a quarter to help take inventory

INSTEAD, put something like this:

- RECONCILED CASH RECEIPTS and prepared daily bank deposits
  - Trained new employees
  - Tasked to maintain customer satisfaction, quality control, and product inventory

IT's all about how you sell yourself. The best way to think about it, is that you are trying to sound a little fancy and impressive. The best idea is to utilize a combination of Fiverr.com and Canva.com. Hire someone to make you a resume who can add some sizzle to the descriptions of past jobs, then create it yourself. Take what they wrote and format the resume as you see fit and save it so you can edit it later. I believe it's best to hire someone to create your resume because even if you can make a better one, they may give you ideas on how to better sell your skills.

I would create two resumes, one that is graphically attractive to human eyes and easy to read, and another that will pass the Applicant Tracking System or ATS for short. The ATS is software used by larger companies and recruiters during the hiring process. Often when applying to a company using ATS if your resume isn't formatted correctly, it might not even get to a hiring manager before being rejected by the program. And while this seems unfair, it can work to your advantage. Imagine you are a large corporation receiving 100's or even 1000's of resumes for a job, wouldn't you want some way to weed out some of them before the search begins? That's what ATS does, and so a having an ATS friendly resume will only benefit you allowing you to avoid competing against the dummies that didn't buy this book!

When you're applying to smaller companies I often believe the best strategy is to make a resume that's attractive and stands out. Either way, you initial resume should just be a template and each time you apply to a new job make sure that you use some of the important keywords that are contained in the job posting. Ensure that previous jobs speak to the current job in some way and rephrase them if you have to.

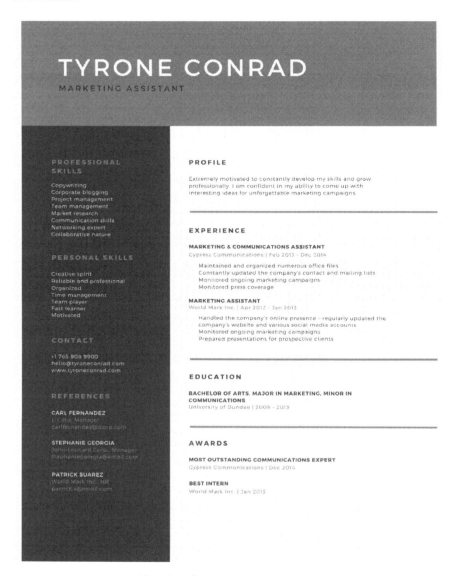

TYRONE CONRAD
MARKETING ASSISTANT

PROFESSIONAL SKILLS

Copywriting
Corporate blogging
Project management
Team management
Market research
Communication skills
Networking expert
Collaborative nature

PERSONAL SKILLS

Creative spirit
Reliable and professional
Organized
Time management
Team player
Fast learner
Motivated

CONTACT

+1 765 908 9900
hello@tyroneconrad.com
www.tyroneconrad.com

REFERENCES

CARL FERNANDEZ
L Corp. Manager
carlfernandez@corp.com

STEPHANIE GEORGIA
John-Leonard Corp., Manager
stephaniegeorgia@email.com

PATRICK SUAREZ
World Mark Inc., HR
patricks@email.com

PROFILE

Extremely motivated to constantly develop my skills and grow professionally. I am confident in my ability to come up with interesting ideas for unforgettable marketing campaigns.

EXPERIENCE

MARKETING & COMMUNICATIONS ASSISTANT
Cypress Communications | Feb 2013 - Dec 2014

Maintained and organized numerous office files
Constantly updated the company's contact and mailing lists
Monitored ongoing marketing campaigns
Monitored press coverage

MARKETING ASSISTANT
World Mark Inc. | Apr 2012 - Jan 2013

Handled the company's online presence – regularly updated the company's website and various social media accounts
Monitored ongoing marketing campaigns
Prepared presentations for prospective clients

EDUCATION

BACHELOR OF ARTS, MAJOR IN MARKETING, MINOR IN COMMUNICATIONS
University of Dundee | 2009 - 2013

AWARDS

MOST OUTSTANDING COMMUNICATIONS EXPERT
Cypress Communications | Dec 2014

BEST INTERN
World Mark Inc. | Jan 2013

Here is a Canva example resume

PHYLLIS SCHWAIGER
COLLEGE STUDENT

Home: 123-456-7890
Mobile: 123-456-7890
hello@reallygreatsite.com
www.reallygreatsite.com
123 Anywhere Street, Any City,
State, Country 12345

EXECUTIVE SUMMARY

I am a 20-year-old history major aspiring to become one of the columnists for the university's official school publication. I am skilled in news writing.

SPECIALIZATIONS

- Journalistic Writing
- Literary Writing
- History
- Political Science
- Theater
- Reading Comprehension
- Play Production
- Reporting
- Public Speaking

WORK EXPERIENCE

Junior Copywriter
Shaw & Sons Copy Inc. | 2019 - Present
- Writes informative copies for international clients
- Brainstorms new copywriting templates twice a month
- Comes up with new ideas for the company website

Junior English Tutor
Beechtown Preschool | 2018 - 2019
- Taught grade school students twice a week
- Helped students prepare for long examinations
- Came up with lesson plans for all english tutors

EDUCATION HIGHLIGHTS

San Dias University
BA Communication | 2016 - Present
- President, SDU School Paper Committee
- Member, The Art Club of San Dias
- Class President
- Gold Medalist, The SDU Feature Writing Contest

Pedigon High School
Class Valedictorian | 2012 - 2016
- Head Photographer, Pedigon High School Daily
- President, The PHS Snap Club
- Member, PHS Circle of Artists
- Scholar, PHS Student Foundation

LANGUAGES SPOKEN

European:	Dutch, Irish, German, Italian, Spanish, Slovenian, Greek, Finnish, and Danish
Asian:	Chinese, Korean, Japanese, Vietnamese, Thai and Filipino

Here is a another Canva example resume

Pro-tip: Set up a LinkedIn account. Hire someone from Fiverr.com to make it look polished and professional. You can hire one person who will do both your resume and

LinkedIn profile for you. Otherwise, wait till you receive back your resume. Give the person designing your LinkedIn profile your brand new resume and the Word document you created with all the relevant details.

Step 3: Visit Fiverr.com to Hire a Professional Cover Letter Creator

Again, spend the time to find the best cover letter creator you can find on the site. Hire them to create a custom cover letter for each of the five different jobs you have chosen. You can always use the same provider that created your resume, but this is completely up to you. Once you receive it, look through it for any errors and make sure it sounds great. Add to it if there is anything else that you think it could use, make sure you don't unintentionally make it worse by your additions. I would ask a few friends and also some older people to look it over and give you feedback. While you're at it, let your friends know about this book and how it's helped your job hunt.

Pro-tip: I like to add a little humor to mine since the hiring manager is likely reading many cover letters and you want to stand out. For instance, I once applied to a sales job for an international chocolate company and I was only 18. I wasn't really qualified, but my cover letter used humor and I had a great interview. Rather than make the same old cover letter that most people do, I told an interesting story.

I mentioned in my letter that I have loved chocolate since I was a little child. At one point my mother stopped letting me drink chocolate milk because she didn't think it was good for me. In response, I wrote a letter to the Chocolate Manufactures Association of America and explained my situation. They wrote back to my mother with a giant packet of information, including scientific research to back my claims for more chocolate, coupons, chocolate samples, and a letter from the Association's president pleading on my behalf.

Needless to say, I could have chocolate whenever I wanted from that point forward. That interesting and funny story got me in the door for an interview. When I asked why I got the interview, they said it was because my cover letter made them laugh. That interview led to an outstanding job that would't have been possible without a winning cover letter.

YOUR COVER LETTER should have the following qualities:

• SHOWS A GLIMPSE of your personality
  • Shows that glimpse in a way that conveys value (my story showed great initiative and determination for a young child)
  • Follows conventional cover letter etiquette
  • Isn't too long
  • Is industry specific (each of the 5 choices you apply to should have a unique cover letter)

NOW YOU HAVE an exceptional looking resume and custom cover letters for each of the jobs you're interested in. You also have a word document that you can refer to when filling out applications both online and in person with all pertinent information about past jobs and experiences. Now it's time to put the finishing touches on your professional appearance before you apply.

————

Finishing Touches (DO NOT SKIP)

Clean up your social media

OKAY, now it's time to make sure you have a consistent professional presence online and off. The first step for this is cleaning up all your social media. This is simple. You either make your social media, private or remove any posts or pictures that you wouldn't want your high school principal to see. This means no pictures of you drunk or partying at a bar. Get rid of political or controversial posts. A nice rule of thumb is to remove posts that caused any disagreement between people on your accounts. If you can make your account private, that's your best bet. Doing that would save you from anything you may miss. There might be something that a potential employer may see. It could be the grammar and slang on your posts that don't match the professional resume and cover letter you presented them.

Create a LinkedIn account

I hope you took my advice in the last section and had a LinkedIn account professionally made. If not, at the very least, create one yourself. Ask a friend to take a professional-looking picture with a collared shirt. Populate your previous work experience on the page. Then connect with anyone you worked with in the past. Next, seek industry-specific groups you could follow. This shows potential employers you care about the industry and job you're applying to work in. Check out profiles that look well crafted and try to emulate what makes them great. A word of caution is that on LinkedIn, unlike other social media, when you view someone's profile they see that.

Create a New Email Address

It's time to create and begin using a new email address. This is what you will use for all future job applications and correspondence with potential employers. I would recommend a Gmail account for ease of use and accessibility of apps. Google offers word processing, spreadsheets, and cloud storage within the mail service itself and also as apps on your phone. In the cloud storage you could keep your resume and document you created earlier with all your previous job information and references. In Google spreadsheets, you could put in all the spreadsheets we've already worked on. This will make it less daunting to apply for jobs. Thus you'll apply for more and increase your chances of landing something perfect. Best of all, since this is a new email address, you will not have any spam mail. You won't have to worry about potential job offers getting lost. Be sure to give yourself access to this from your smartphone through whatever mail app you use. Be sure to check this often to avoid missing any potential opportunities.

Send Test Emails

With your new email address, send out copies of your resume and cover letter to your old email address. Look over those to ensure that they are sending correctly. If not, be sure to revise it and test it again to ensure that it looks perfect.

Dress the Part

Now comes the fun part, learning how to dress for an interview.

If you have questions about how to dress, the simplest answer would be to do a web search. For guys, the general rule of thumb would be to own at least one basic black suit, nice matching black dress shoes, and a shirt and tie that match. I managed a suit store as one of my earlier careers. I can tell you from experience what a difference a suit can make on a man. Be sure to have matching socks and always wear a belt. Women have more options with what to wear, however they will tell you that's not always a good thing. I'm a man and won't pretend to have the best idea of what women should wear for interviews. I would recommend you try your best to find out what's considered appropriate dress for that industry. Then take the time to ask a few trusted friends if they believe your outfit choice is appropriate. You will always want your interview outfit to be on the conservative side.

Start Applying To Jobs

So now comes the fun part, sitting in front of your computer for days on end and applying to every single job you can. Your prospective jobs should rank from 1 to 5, so start with your top choice. Here come the spreadsheets again. Since you made it this far, we will not drop the ball at the one-yard line. We will use the same five job search engines used earlier. Then, we will update the spreadsheets after each submitted application. The spreadsheets should contain the following columns:

1. Company
2. Address
3. Commute time
4. Salary (if known)
5. Company Benefits

I know what you're thinking, by now you're sick of spreadsheets and I don't blame you. I'm sick of typing the word spreadsheets in this book. But for the sake of your future, remember that all this work will pay off. Staying organized and being thorough might be enough to land you the job of your dreams. If you're familiar with the companies in the job market, make a list. Start with the one you'd most like to work for all the way to the one that you least like to work for. Take my advice on this. Apply to everything. This will give you leverage and practice for future interviews and negotiations. Some jobs on the job search engines will be scams, so don't include them. The reason I say to apply to everything is twofold. First, you will gain valuable experience during your interviews. Second, you may receive many jobs offers. You can leverage these offers against each other during salary negotiations. Remember, the starting salary you make today affects the salary you make for the rest of your lifetime. Applying to everything and taking multiple job interviews gives you a better understanding of what working in this industry will be like. That may inform your decisions for the future.

So the initial step is applying to the jobs you see on the search engines. After each application that you submit, add it to your spreadsheet. Be sure to fill out each column of the spreadsheet as best you can. The hope is that after submitting enough resumes and cover letters, you will receive several offers. You'll use the spreadsheet to help you decide which option might be the best for you. You must go with your gut and use your judgment should multiple offers arrive.

Pro Tip: Remember, don't apply to jobs that are farther than 30 miles away unless you won't mind that commute. Remember in some cities commutes are measured in minutes and not miles. An example would be something like New York City. You wouldn't want a 30-mile commute and may not even want a 3-mile commute.

Try to complete applications to every job that you can in your first job choice within one week. You may find that this is a full-time gig itself, but buckle down and keep applying. If you are in a major metropolitan area, there could be a thousand openings. In situations like this, it's important to spend the time upfront to rank the firms you wish to work for. Start applying from the top down.

Once you've spent a week applying to all the jobs within your first choice, you can take a break for a few days. See if there's any interest before moving on to your second job choice. If you're in a rush, apply to your second job choice right away and don't stop till you finish all the choices. If you're unable to submit to everything within a week, stick with it before moving on to a lower-tier job choice. Repeat this until you've either gotten a job or exhausted the first five job choices you picked. If by this time you're not receiving much interest, you will need to decide if there's something wrong. The first thing to investigate is if you're applying to entry-level jobs. Check if you sent your resume correctly. Then ensure your cover letter is the way you wanted it to look. If everything is going out as it should, it may be time to move out your top five choices. Move into your list of 20 and begin applying to those.

Pro-tip: I recommend reaching back out via email to the employers you are especially excited to work for after two weeks. Be polite, thank them for considering your resume, focus on what would make you a good fit, ask questions you might have, and keep it short. If you are unsure about how to write this search online for examples.

Now it's time for the fun part, getting ready for all the job interviews!

how to double your job callbacks in 48 hours

. . .

SINCE YOUR RESUME is most likely short on substance, it's time to add some filler. To do this, look at online job postings for the jobs you seek and see what skills they talk about, require and recommend. Make a list of as many skills as you see for each of the five jobs you are seeking. These could include anything but for this example let's say you want to get a job in marketing. I would begin by searching for free marketing certifications and see what comes up.

Boom! One of the first things I spot is a blog post about *6 Free Marketing Certifications That Will Boost Your Credibility.* Just like that, you have a list of 6 resume builders that most likely will take less than a day. If a web search yields nothing applicable, start going down the list of skills the jobs require and search for free certifications for each.

Now I know what you are thinking. How good could a free certification even be? The answer is, it doesn't matter. Any certification puts you ahead of the guy who didn't spend the 1.5 hours to get it. The trick is that if we can fill up some blank space on your resume with things that show drive and initiative, a company will be more willing to take a chance on you.

Short job board aptitude tests are another recent development that may work to your advantage. You now can take tests that can show up on your profile on a few of the more popular job hunting sites, and I recommend you take advantage of that. The reason is that most of these tests are easy if you have a basic understanding of the subject. They often only take 15 minutes or less, and since you are doing this on your own, there is no pressure. Another benefit is that often you can take them again and again while only posting your highest score. Best of all, many of the jobs you will apply too will ask you to take the tests as part of your resume submission, and by doing it ahead of time you ensure that they only receive your best score. That way when you apply for a job, the site will notify them of you "expert" status in the skill they are testing. It's just one more way to build credibility to your resume and increase your chances.

So over the next two days, complete as many simple free certifications as you can along with any applicable tests. If you see any paid certifications and wish to spend the money, go ahead, but often there are enough quality free certifications. Find them from the most direct and reputable sources you can. By the time you finish, you have several more items that you can add to your resume to help you stand out from the crowd. Print the certifications out and be sure to include the certification number on any applications.

If you are trying to get a job that has no free certifications available, take a Microsoft Office or leadership certification and throw that on the resume. It's better than nothing and you can be sure the person posting the jobs is familiar with MS Office, even if it has nothing to do with your career choice. Again, something is always better than nothing.

how to ace a job interview

· · ·

NOW COMES everybody's favorite part — job interviews. For some people, job interviews are something they look forward to and don't get too nervous about. Others avoid job interviews like the plague. Job interviews are somewhere between those two extremes. By nature, job interviews are nerve-racking ordeals. They test how you react to new surroundings when under pressure. In fact, there are still companies out there that love to ask impossible questions. They attempt to get inside your head and discover how you analyze problems to reach a solution. Here are some examples below:

"DESCRIBE the color yellow to someone who's blind." — Spirit Airlines

"IF YOU WERE ASKED to unload a 747 full of jelly beans, what would you do?" — Bose

· · ·

"WHO WOULD WIN in a fight between Spiderman and Batman?" — Stanford University[10]

THOSE QUESTIONS ARE NOT MEANT to make you feel stupid, but to test your logic and reasoning skills. The good news is, more companies are moving away from these types of questions. They are going back to the more traditional questions that you may be more familiar with. We can't prepare for unanswerable questions, but we can prepare for the common ones.

Know What They Are Looking For

Before you begin the series of interviews, put yourself on the best footing by knowing how you will answer common questions you're likely to hear. Do an online search for interview questions. Visit several websites to make sure you have a decent list. I won't bother trying to compile this list myself. There are many websites that list hundreds of common questions. They also have also tips on answering them. My only advice for you here is to write each question down in your notebook. Take the time to jot down a quick answer that you would give in an interview. You're trying to convey to the interviewer your dedication, hard work, and responsibility. Here is what the person interviewing you and their company is looking for:

• **THEY WANT to know you won't embarrass them**
  • **They want to know you will make them look good rather than look foolish to their bosses**
  • **They want to know past employers and managers were happy with you**
  • **They want to know you get along with others**

- **They want to know you plan to stick around**
- **They want to know you are reliable**
- **They want to know you are honest**
- **They want to know you are eager to learn their systems**
- **They want to know you can help them out in a pinch**
- **They want to know you're eager to grow with the company**

LET'S go over each one of these points. Try to remember that during the interview, each of your answers should convey these things in different ways. Once you learn to weave those qualities into your answers, you will ace most job interviews. But the trick is to answer subtly and perfect the art of alleviating those hiring fears. Often they may not even know or understand these fears. Do this and you will land the job even when you are not the most qualified candidate.

They want to know you won't embarrass them

The people interviewing you fear embarrassment. They worry that if they hire you and you fail, they will be accountable for it. You need to provide them with the justification they need to go to bat for you with the company. Your interview needs to be strong. Make this person vouch for you when it's time to pick the last candidate for the position.

They want to know you will make them look good rather than look foolish to their bosses

Depending on the job, you may interview with several people. But at one point or another, you will usually interview with your direct supervisor. This supervisor wants to know that you have their back and you will stick up for them when they make a mistake. They want to know you'll be loyal and that you would never speak ill of them. They want to know that you make excellent choices. They want to make sure they will not get called into meetings because they took a chance on hiring you.

They want to know past employers and managers are happy with you

This can be an easy one for you to get right. Rule of thumb is to never speak negatively about past employers, managers, or co-workers. Even if you left your last job because your supervisor was an idiot, never say that in an interview. Your answer should reflect that you left because you're looking for more growth. You can always say you're looking for a challenge. Anything is fine, but never say that people you worked with in the past sucked. Say that you learned new things because of that opportunity.

They want to know you get along with others

This ties into the last one. They want to know you get along with all your co-workers. You need to express to them you don't cause drama and you do your job with a smile. A negative person can bring down morale. So this is your chance to express that you could work with negative people and even help them improve. Once again, this is your chance to let them know you get along with everyone and you won't rock the boat.

They want to know you plan to stick around

According to Forbes, "Approximately $1,200 was spent per employee"[11] in workplace training. This means that a company is investing in you in both time and money. Like any investment, you want to know it will pay off and the hiring manager is no different. They want to know that you're not looking to job hop from one opportunity to another. They want someone loyal to the company. By now, you're realizing that perceived loyalty is a big factor in interviews. Make sure you express that you plan to stick around for the long term — even if you are not sure that's the case. Who knows? You might start this job and find out you enjoy it. Maybe even receive unexpected advancement opportunities.

They want to know you are reliable

Do you show up to work on time? Do you call in sick or take personal days? Do you have a vehicle or reliable transportation you can depend on? During your interview, you need to express that you are reliable, punctual and that you don't miss work.

They want to know you are honest

Have you worked with cash registers or bank deposits in the past, no matter how small, at other jobs? Make sure they know you worked around money in the past and are trustworthy. You will not get hired by anyone if you don't appear to be honest. Dishonesty includes stealing company time, i.e. taking too long of breaks or showing up late. If you have any examples of past employers trusting you with something of value or importance, tell them. Be sure to include how that past employer was rewarded for their trust in you.

They want to know you are eager to learn their systems

Every company likes to do things their way and they're not interested in changing how they do things. At the start of your career, refrain from giving advice or critiques. As you progress in your career, you may find the company is not only willing to take your advice but are eager to hear it. However, in the beginning and straight out of school they're not interested in your ideas and opinions on anything. Let them know that you're eager to learn the way this company does things. Show them you are not too arrogant to think you have a better way.

I once interviewed a woman for a position who repeatedly gave suggestions about things my company was doing wrong that she would do differently. And while her thoughts were valid, I knew right away she wasn't getting a call back. She lacked the social intelligence to understand her feedback was a critique on the one interviewing her. Be humble and open to doing things the way it's done, unless they specifically ask you to shake things up.

They want to know you can help them out in a pinch

Can you come in early? Can you stay late? Can you come in on the weekends? Can you come in on your day off? The answer is yes; better yet, let them know these things before they even ask. If you live close, now is your chance to let them know that. Say that you're only a five-minute drive away. Tell them your past employers always valued your ability to help them out in a pinch. Make sure they know that they can count on you should they ever need to.

They want to know you're eager to grow with the company

They want to know that you're eager to grow with the company. This one can be tricky depending on the size of the company you're interviewing for. Sometimes growth could mean taking the interviewer's job. Use your best judgment here. Express your willingness to learn and take on extra responsibilities as needed. During your career, you'll find that more responsibilities means more money. The more you can do, the more valuable you are to the company and the harder you are to replace. During the interview, you need to tell them you enjoy being someone others can count on when things are tough. Let the interviewer know that in past jobs you have always been the one co-workers and supervisors turned too in a pinch.

Research the Company and Industry

Before your interview, make sure you have a thorough knowledge of what the company does. Make sure you're familiar with the industry that you will work in. Also, read any recent or major news articles about your company. Visit their social media pages. Your interviewer wants to know that you're knowledgeable about current events. Tell them you are interested in the industry beyond just a paycheck. They will also want to know the reason you sought this company versus another. It's important that you're familiar with where the company has been and where it may go. Reference recent things you've read about the industry and company during your interview.

Print Out the Job Description

Before each interview that you go on, be sure to print out the job description. Highlight specific skills they are looking for. If there are any keywords or phrases you're unfamiliar with, research them ahead of time. Use those keywords and phrases during the interview to pack the maximum punch.

Night Before and Day of the Interview

Make sure you plan your outfit the night before. Everything

you plan to wear should be clean and wrinkle-free. Make sure you know the proper address of where you're going and you mapped out how long it'll take to get there. Plan to arrive at your interview location 10-15 minutes early. But do not head inside for the interview earlier than 10 minutes before it's scheduled to begin. Use this time to jot down a few questions you may ask during the interview. These questions should answer something you want to know. Present yourself as an asset to the company (be subtle). Put your phone on silent and be sure anything you might need to access from it is on a printed piece of paper. Do not take your phone out again until you're back in your car after the interview. While you are waiting in the lobby, review the job description, cover letter, resume and notes **do not use your phone**. The single act of looking professional and not scrolling on your phone will make an impression and separate you from most other potential candidates.

Be sure to smile at everyone you encounter on the company's property and treat everyone with respect. You never know who you might have walked past on the way to the interview room. This includes while driving on the company property. You would hate to cut off your potential boss while driving in the parking lot. Throughout the interview, smile and maintain eye contact. At the conclusion of the interview, ask about the next steps.

Bring:
* Five Copies of Resume
* Five Copies of Cover Letter
* Notebook
* Pen
* The Google doc that contains references and past volunteer work

bonus: all about the side hustle

. . .

AHH YES, the ever elusive perfect side hustle. A way to make good money during your free time while not spending all your energy or distracting from your actual career. If only it were that simple. While side hustles are fantastic, they can also quickly drain us of our drive and energy to perform optimally at our everyday job. A side hustle can be many activities and trust me, I have done a lot of them. Im going to discuss some of the most common and then tell you about some less common ones that might also be a perfect fit for your lifestyle. Mostly, these can be done anywhere and are not location specific as to not exclude any readers. Below is a list of what I consider being the best side hustles:

• **DATA ENTRY** - BORING but companies all over the world need someone to move information from one spreadsheet to another. This has the bonus of providing you with something to place on your resume and could even lead to some advancement if you choose the right company. The average entry pay for data entry work is between \$11 - \$15 an hour and can grow incrementally as you prove yourself.

• **VIRTUAL ASSISTANT** - PEOPLE and companies all around the world like use websites like Upwork.com to find a virtual assistant that could do anything from schedule appointments, light internet research and document creation. Upwork.com is nice because it allows you to set up a profile and bid on jobs being offered. It also allows prospective employers to view your profile and message you about opportunities. For one off gigs that don't require you jumping through hoops of virtual job auditions, Fiverr.com is more than capable of providing steady income. The downside being that you need to set a good system and procedure in place since you will work with various gig buyers under strict deadlines. For any online job sites like these, try to research the most active members and see what they are doing to stand out and what others are looking for. Best of all, you set the rates and can increase them as you improve your skills and gain more experience.

• **TUTOR** - Now I won't get into the shady underbelly of getting paid to write papers and take tests for high school and college students, but tutoring can be a lucrative and gratifying opportunity. This is especially great for someone who plans to enter the teaching profession or perhaps aspires to be a supervisor, since you can reference your ability to tutor on your resume. Almost every college and university offers tutoring to students by students. In addition, there are many companies like Tutor.com where you can build a profile and provide your service. You can also advertise in local publications, Facebook community boards, Reddit, and classified if you wish to work privately. On average, the starting pay for a tutor is

$15 an hour, and the sky is the limit if you have a track record of helping others. Parents will pay just about anything to give their children a leg up in their academics.

- **RIDE-SHARING** - GOT A CAR, a license, and haven't committed murder? You can probably find a job driving for Uber or Lyft. The jury is still out on how lucrative this is when factoring in fuel and general wear and tear, but it is a solid option.

Pro-tip: If you work evenings at a restaurant job or something similar, you can spray on a little cologne and start picking up riders as soon as your shift ends. When I lived in LA, I would do this after I got out of work at 2am and would routinely make $100 a night driving drunks around till about 4am. Best of all, anyone who works in the restaurant biz knows that you wired for a few hours after your shift and wouldn't be able to sleep, anyway. In fact, working for a ride-share company probably doubles your earnings if you factor in forgoing the booze you might consume to forget about annoying customers you had throughout the day. I do not recommend ride-sharing after your normal day job for most people. Nothing would be worse than picking up a co-worker or your boss and having them tell the office you're a good taxi driver the next day. That said if you need to make money, you gotta do what you gotta do.

- **FOOD DELIVERY** - WANT to pay off your student loans and don't care how you do it? Deliver pizzas for your local pizza shop and watch your bank account grow. It's not super lucrative, but if you receive fair pay from the shop, tips from the customers, some free food at the end of the night, it's not so bad. Just don't eat a slice of customer pizza, even though its glorious pepperoni scent is filling up the interior of your car (trust me, they will know). Since it's the modern era, there are also companies like PostMates and Uber Eats among others that allow you to deliver from a variety of restaurants in your area.

• **Do tasks for others** - Sites like TaskRabbit allow others to do the things they are too lazy, stupid, or unable to do themselves. This could be anything from setting up furniture to running for groceries, but in most cases it's not to challenging and can make you decent money in your free time. Best of all, it's not an ongoing commitment and you can work or not depending on your schedule. Pay varies depending on tasks.

• **PHOTOGRAPHY** - GOT a $1000+ camera and like to take pictures? Are you willing to learn complex editing software needed to make people look skinnier, nicer, and just plain better? If so photography can be a very lucrative side hustle that can easily turn into your main hustle. The trick is starting slow and building out a portfolio doing work for low to no money for friends, family, and acquaintances. Build a simple website with a provider like Squarespace and show off your beautiful work. If you can get people to share your work on Facebook, Instagram, and other visually heavy social media platforms you might find yourself with more work than you can handle. The holidays are especially lucrative time with people willing to fork over hard earned money for just 30 minutes of your time. Everyone wants to impress their families with the perfect holiday card. Don't want to spend money up front on a camera? There are plenty of sites that rent them for a week or more at a time and allow you to try before you buy. Don't wait too long as that can add up quick with most places charging at least $100 for a weekly rental.

• **AIRBNB** - GOT a spare room or a spare house? Either get a roommate or rent it out and start making that glorious side hustle cash for almost nothing. Look at other local hosts in the area. See what they are charging, offering, and how their photos look online. Copy the best and if you are just starting out price it a little more competitively to get some positive reviews. Really try to wow the guests because these days, a bed and a hot shower just doesn't cut it. Many customers expect the red carpet treatment too and will rate you accordingly.

Pro-tip: This is a great time to test out your brand new photography skills and get real life feedback in the form of bookings. If not, find a friend to take professional photos as people will not stay at a place that's poorly photographed.

• **SOCIAL MEDIA and Reputation Management for Small Business -** Have a friend who owns their own business and might let you handle their social media accounts? Take a course on Udemy.com on professional social media management, tell them you took the course, then ask if they would let you manage it for a 3 month trial period. All they have to do is pay for the cost of advertisements. Make sure they pony up for the ads and begin practicing A/B testing of ads on various networks and tracking results. The keys to this side hustle is to under promise and over deliver. Small and medium-sized business owners often think that just because they are finally spending a few bucks advertising, the floodgates will open and customers will pour in. That's not usually the case, and social media takes about 3 months of time and energy investment before it pays off. This is not the side hustle for someone looking for easy, fast cash, but it can be lucrative once you establish a reputation as someone who gets results. After you work on a friend's business page for a few months, head over to appsumo.com and see if they have any tools that will help you work more effectively. Apps on that website often charge a one time fee of under $50 for lifetime use of a product that is just coming to market. All apps on that site are vetted then customer rated to ensure that it does what it says. Appsumo.com also offers a money back guarantee. You will also want to familiarize yourself with canva.com which will help you do light graphic design work and social posts. Once you buy a few tools, get yourself a nice business card and a cheap LLC and start working to build a brand. Again this is not quick, easy, or cheap, but this can be lucrative if you stick with it and develop a good plan to secure more clients.

• **WORK FOR TIPS** - Not sure if I even count this as a side hustle, but waiting tables, bartending, or bussing in the restaurant industry are reliable ways to make some quick cash. The work sucks, but sometimes you have decent co-workers and free shift beer. Also, it improves your social skills and helps you learn to start micro-conversations. Best of all, you get feedback at how well you converse with people in the form of tips. As I have said before, working for tips is the best training for sales that you can ever hope for. Restaurants are not the only source of tips either. Often hotels in your area might have valet staff or bellman who also make lucrative money in season. Another option is working on a golf course or tennis club. Be creative and you can find a cash heavy service industry job that might be just what you need.

• **COOKING -** I WOULDN'T RECOMMEND WORKING in a restaurant kitchen, and if you know anyone who does, they will tell you the same. High stress, low pay and terrible hours are just some reasons. But, if you are a decent cook, you might find someone who would hire you to meal prep or cook meals for them on a regular or semi-regular basis.

• **CLEANING -** Admittedly not the most glamorous job but every town has a hoarder or two in it and you might be just the answer to their prayers! But, if cleaning up a decade's worth of someone's random filth isn't your idea of a good time, hotels are always hiring housekeepers to clean after the guests check out. There are also overnight cleaning positions for offices that aren't as filthy as other places you might clean. If you are looking for a way to break into this side hustle visit care.com and see how it works. They are one of the largest databases for private housekeepers.

• **BABYSIT/NANNY/ELDER Care -** This can be a fun and lucrative side hustle if you enjoy children. If you prove yourself indispens-able to the family, you may even find yourself invited on family vacations to watch the children so the parents can have a little downtime. This can start fast and grow quickly, especially if you grow your skills and certifications to stand out from the competition. Take a CPR class and a few basic safety certifications and you can add that to your resume. Perhaps a cooking class or two and you can find more elusive jobs like live-in nanny that can also save you rent. The choice is yours, but the opportunities are abundant if you don't mind dealing with loud screaming children all day. Conversely, you can look for senior care opportunities and spend time with someone who has the wisdom and experience of many decades. Either way, you might find yourself changing diapers. Senior care jobs are more permanent opportunities, since families like to find one person who they feel comfortable with and stick with them. If you are looking for a way to break into this side hustle, again my recommendation is to visit care.com and see how it works. They are one of the largest databases for child care.

• **Dog Walking/Sitting** - Much like working as a nanny but without most of the headache. If you love animals this is definitely a side hustle to consider. This can be done regularly or on a case-by-case basis through apps. One thing to remember is if you are working a 9-5 job you will probably miss most opportunities as people want you to stop by their homes and let their dogs out during those hours. As for the sitting portion of this, you might get to crash in pleasant houses with a fridge full of food and HBO in exchange for hanging out with some fun dogs all day and night! The best part is you get paid at the end. I will reference care.com once again as it is an excellent source for dog walking and sitting leads.

• **Teach Language** - If you are a native English speaker, you may have hit the lottery and not realized it yet. As a fluent English speaker, you can help people around the world learn a second language. Often a degree is required for many of the online

English tutoring gigs, but not always. You could also advertise private tutoring in places like China, where the demand for learning English is huge. Often the pay starts at $20 an hour moving up and the sky is the limit if you teach privately. You can do a simple online search for companies hiring as they change frequently. If I were you, I would visit Appsumo.com, find some good video conference software and buy a lifetime deal. I would then figure out what steps I need to take to comply with Chinese laws, buy cheap advertising space, and start putting together a class with 20-30 students. Charge them $2-$10 each class depending on length of class and how organized you are. It might take a little while, but if you can get referrals, are responsible and easy to work with for the parents and students, and reliable you might soon be swimming in a sea of Yuan.

• **WASH AND DETAIL Cars** - If you enjoy cars and have a mild to severe case of OCD, this might be a great opportunity for you. Car dealerships are always looking for people to help them wash a detail cars in their lot, because no one wants to buy a new car with old bird poop on it. You could stick there and perhaps learn more about working at a dealership in another capacity one day. Or you could take what you learn and open a mobile detailing company by advertising your services locally online. Dealerships are not the only ones hiring either, body shops and professional detailers often need help and if you plan to go it alone one day, I recommend learning on someone else's dime first. That's actually my recommendation in life when you want to learn anything.

• **PET GROOMING** - AGAIN, this is a perfect job for those who enjoy animals. You can start by searching for pet groomers in the area and see if they need help. If hired you can earn a few bucks while you learn the trade, but the big money comes from doing it for yourself. Pet people are a crazy lot and most of them like to swerve their car to miss hitting a squirrel in the road than you. So if you can prove your skills and make their beloved "children" beautiful, you can charge a premium. It takes a little know how, a few tools, and the ability to handle getting bit for a Chihuahua now and then. If you do this on your own for the premium pay, I would recommend looking into forming an LLC and getting insurance as you don't want to be the one holding the bag, so to speak if a pet dies on your watch.

• **FREELANCE WRITER** - If you are the sicko who enjoyed English class and cringes at poor grammar, you may be the perfect candidate for freelance writing. In this internet age, you can easily find people needing blog posts, news articles, books and just about everything in between. Best of all, if you can learn the skills of SEO, you can charge extra for articles and blog posts someone will put online. As with most things in life at the beginning, the pay grows with experience and examples of past projects. This is perhaps one of the easiest side hustles to earn money from. However, ask any author and they will tell you that writing day in and day out requires a certain amount of mental gymnastics to complete on a deadline.

• **PERSONAL TRAINING** - GOT A KILLER BOD? If so, check out personal training as a side hustle. The wonderful thing about now is that most people are fat, yet media and society tell us we need to be skinny. That's the perfect combination for a steady stream of potential clients. To really advance in the field, you need to be certified. NCCA is the most respected in the industry, however there are perhaps dozens of personal training certifications and chances are your clients won't be as familiar as you are with them. My thoughts are any certification is better than none, and you can always gain additional certifications later. So grab a certification and brush up on your human anatomy before you begin. After that, find a local gym that will bring you on and let you get a little practice under your belt. Next you can consider branching out and offering private training sessions for more money or continue to hone your skills and get paid at the gym. Your pay is limited only by how much people think you're worth, so a six-pack, a wall of certifications and some good referrals will go a long way in boosting your bottom line.

• **MUSIC LESSONS** - For those with a musical ear and some vocal or instrumental talent, you could consider offering private music lessons. If you will travel to people's houses you can charge more, but if you prefer to work from home, you can have students come to you. This also has the added benefit of helping to keep your own musical skills sharp, too.

• **WRITE RESUMES** - DID you make your own resume and enjoy it? Perhaps this is a skill others would pay you for? Advertise your resume skills online with examples (don't put anyone's personal information on your example resumes). Search online for places to offer that service, Fiverr.com is probably a good place to start. All you really need is some decent word processing software, google docs, or canva.com resume templates and you are off and running. Research trigger words and colors that hiring managers like to see and be sure to incorporate them. This will also help you practice perfecting your own resume, which is never a bad skill to have.

· · ·

• **HOUSE SIT** - People travel all the time for work or vacation, and sometimes they like someone monitoring things while they're gone. It may be as simple as dropping in each day and bringing in the mail. However, it could also be as difficult as watering the plants, mowing the lawn, taking care of the pets and spending the night. No matter what the responsibilities are make sure they are communicated clearly, and they pay you fairly. Also, unless they tell you it's ok to dip into the booze, eat the food, or have people over, it's best to avoid that. The neighbors will let them know about the kegger you throw and dozen delivered pizzas.

• **INTERIOR DECORATING** - If you have a creative eye and can transform drab into fab, consider a side hustle as an interior decorator. Explore the website and app houzz.com and look at what is popular in the decorating space. Then create a profile and begin advertising your services. You may need to do a few projects on the cheap to build your portfolio, but word of mouth goes a long way in this profession. Everyone likes to show off their new home and if you can wow people, they will be happy to tell their friends about you.

• **ONLINE MOCK JURIES** - We live in a very litigious society these days and with reputations on the line, lawyers don't want to leave anything to chance. Lawyers like to prepare for trial using mock juries when possible to avoid surprises they might encounter when presenting in front of real juries. You can often work from home and receive anywhere from $20 and up per case. Your per hour pay is very good as a mock juror, however you will not have a steady supply of work so this usually isn't the best side hustle. This is perfect to add to your side hustle mix as an additional income stream. One of the bigger players in the online mock jury world is onlineverdict.com, they have earned a reputation for reliable payment each month.

• **Medical Testing** - *Don't do this* Yes, I will mention medical testing, though I'm not sure how much of a side hustle it is. Unless you live in a major city, it would be tough to find enough tests to give you any steady income, no matter how small. Also avoid this, unless you have very little regard for your own body. I have seen far too many zombie movies to think it's a good idea.

• **Translate** - If you can write and speak in two languages, you can make money in translating. Companies both online and off have needs to translate products and services into other languages for both international and domestic use. And while it might be difficult to find a company that needs to your services if you have no track record, there are many book authors who would take a chance on you if the price is right. I recommend reaching out to small-medium book publishing companies and seeing if they have any translation needs. You can also use sites like Fiverr.com and Upwork.com for both long and short-term translation gigs.

• **Proofreading and Editing**- If you have a keen sense of grammar, syntax and spelling, you might have a successful future in proofreading and editing. Bloggers, authors, publishers and small businesses all need proofreading and editing done to keep their work looking professional. One thing to be clear on is what stage of editing they task you with completing. In traditional editing, there are multiple stages that range from helping develop characters and storyline to checking for spelling and grammatical errors. Be sure you have clear direction about what type of editing they expect you to do and the deadline. Often when working with new writers they will be unfamiliar with the various editing stages and so your job will be to educate them on it and set their expectations accordingly. You can find editing and proofreading work on Upwork.com and Fiverr.com and by contacting publishers, bloggers, and authors. I recommend starting with a very low rate to get practice and experience and raising the rate as your skills and reputation improve.

- **RENT out your car** - This allows you to make a little extra cash without lifting a finger. If you live in a larger city, chances are there is a company willing to pay you to rent your car to strangers. All these companies offer insurance and supposedly vet their customers, but how well is up for debate. If you don't always need your car, this is a good way to earn a few dollars for no work on your part. The companies that are biggest in this field change often, so I won't list any specifics. To find out if this is available in your area, do a web search and find the top 5-10 companies that come up and see what locations they operate in. After that, try to find reviews and decide if it's right for you.

- **BOOK KEEPING** - Every company needs to keep an organized record of their finances, so book keeping is a job that will always be in high demand. The trick is learning how to do it the right way and making sure businesses know they can count on you. You can either be on a company's payroll or work as a freelance bookkeeper. Beware of companies that have no flexibility with their hours. Freelance bookkeepers often set their own rates and charge as much as $60 an hour, which can make this a very lucrative and stable side hustle. While you can find work with no degree most potential employers would prefer a candidate that has at least taken some accounting classes if not gotten and associate's degree. But as with everything in life, a track record and referrals from other businesses can sometimes trump any education requirements.

• **TRANSCRIBING** - This side hustle is one software may soon replace, but while available it's a good one to pursue. This job requires you to take recordings and speeches and convert them to word documents. This is an in demand service within the legal, medical and business fields. There are also many authors and bloggers who use a transcription service to write more efficiently. You can find work in this field on major job boards and freelance work on the usual suspects of Fiverr.com and Upwork.com.

• **LANDSCAPE** - Do you love the smell of fresh cut grass and the get a middle-aged dad grin when you look at a pristine lawn? If so, consider a side hustle as a landscaper and create masterpieces one lawn at a time. While this field is competitive, it is also easy to break into as the service as everyone needs to cut their lawn and trim their bushes. Your most successful advertisement will often be word of mouth, so tell your happy clients to let their friends and family know about you. To really start making some money, you will need some buy some basic gear. Often you can find this used through local classifieds from homeowners who no longer need all their lawn equipment. At a minimum, you will want a large push mower, lawn trimmer, leaf blower, extra gas canisters and a trailer to haul around your gear. A pickup truck and riding lawnmower become requirements as you grow and expand your business. You can advertise your service on social media like Facebook.com, craigslist.com, local classifieds, and print flyers. You might even convince clients to let you put small signs in their yard for a reduced rate. Beware, if you live in cooler climates you will find yourself out of work come winter time. That is why many landscapers also do fall cleanup (leaf and gutter cleaning) and winter snow removal to make ends meet during the slower seasons.

• **VOICE OVER WORK** - Voice over work is a popular side hustle that requires only a few basic things. If you have a decent computer, a good microphone, professional quality headphones, and a quiet place to work you can quickly begin finding gigs in this field. Fiverr.com and Upwork.com are of course popular places to find work online. You can also work with ACX.com or Voices.com to find work creating Audiobooks for publishers and authors. Free software from companies like Audacityteam.org has a bit of a learning curve but allows you to create professional recordings that clients will pay for. Start cheap, under promise, over deliver and keep soliciting new clients and you will quickly find yourself with steady work. As your portfolio grows, so can your paychecks, as you can charge a premium for your successful track record.

THERE YOU HAVE IT, folks! I promised you a book about finding a career and was nice enough to even include an entire chapter on side jobs and side hustles. Now this doesn't include every side hustle, but this contains most of the more common ones. There is enough variety on this list that anyone can find something they want to do in their free time to earn more money and pay off those student loans a little faster.

Back when our parents joined the workforce, it was not unreasonable to assume that you would spend your life with one company and they would take care of you in retirement. Today companies are beholden to the shareholder and bottom line, so it's important that you develop some alternative means of income, even if you never plan on leaving your job. The economy changes and things happen, but if you have some side hustle, it can help you weather the inevitable storm. The key is finding something you enjoy doing and working to perfect your skills during your free time. Think of your side hustle as a hobby that makes you money and you will roll in the dough during the good times and able to continue to pay your bills during the bad!

conclusion

If you made it this far in the book, congratulations! Pat yourself on the back and know that you're so far ahead of your peers. We began this book by discussing problems facing workers across the world. Many of these problems apply to everyone, but these especially affect fresh graduates. The problems are lack of experience, limited financial resources, job automation, and a limited workable skill set. We can overcome all these problems. Now, you already have all the tools you need to make this happen.

We also discussed goal setting and clarifying what we were hoping to achieve. We discussed what success looks like to your family, friends, and peers and why it matters. Afterwards, we discussed what success looks like to you. We discussed why that's the most important measurement. Before you began reading this book, maybe you had not spent the time to decide what you want out of life. We visualized and daydreamed 5, 10 and even 20 years into the future, then checked if our career goals match with those visualizations. We then looked at the motivations that drive us and matched that up with careers that excite us.

We discussed Maslow's hierarchy of needs and how a career

fulfills some of our basic needs in life. If you pick the correct career, you'll be better able to find that true lasting fulfillment. We created several spreadsheets based on researched data. We combined our thoughts and feelings with actionable knowledge. This helps us find the best jobs for our situation. While it took time and effort, you now have a comprehensive database of jobs in your area. These jobs were all ranked according to their ability to fulfill your goals. We narrowed those down further and came up with the five best jobs that we can focus our search on.

You learned the steps to create a resume and cover letter that will get you noticed. You also had them customized according to the jobs you're seeking. You learned what the interviewers are looking for and how to give them what they want. You've made their decision easy. You made it happen by establishing yourself as one of the best candidates for the position. The skills you learned through this book will help you for the rest of your life. You now have the tools to find the best jobs for yourself and ace the job interviews are sure to follow. You even have a few potential side hustles to fall back on to give you some extra spending money when you land your dream job or help make ends meet while you wait for that to materialize. The world is your oyster, and the future is yours. Use what you've learned to achieve what others can only dream of!

If you have enjoyed this book, please consider writing a review. It really does make a difference.

also by jon nelsen

- *Starting a Bed and Breakfast: Bite Sized Interviews With Successful B&B's on Building a Brand That Lasts*

- *Running a Bed and Breakfast: Bite Sized Interviews With Successful B&B's on Maintaining a Thriving Inn*

- *One More Beer, Please (Vol. 1, 2, 3): The Largest Collection of Interviews With Brewmasters and Craft Breweries*

- *Solar Panels: Are Solar Panels Worth It?*

- *Complete Guide to Roofing and Solar: Homeowners Essential Handbook for Money Saving DIY Roof Construction and Solar Panels*

- *What I Wish My Roofer Had Told Me: The Ultimate Guide to the Roof of Your Dreams on a Budget*

- *The Only Time I Set the Bar Low Is for Limbo: Reaching Your Potential in Work, Life, and Relationships*

- *What College Didn't Teach You About Getting Hired: The Ultimate Guide on How to Find a Job*

After Graduation

- *The Anxiety Answer: The Step-by-Step Guide to Overcoming Fears, Phobias, and Other Voices in Your Head*

- *Solar Powered Energy Theft: Legal No Money Down Solar Panels for Homeowners*

references

[1]"Millennials: The Job-Hopping Generation - Gallup." https://www.gallup.com/workplace/231587/millennials-job-hopping-generation.aspx. Accessed 7 Apr. 2020.

[2] "Why is Work Experience Important? | AllAboutCareers." https://www.allaboutcareers.com/careers-advice/work-experi ence/why-is-work-experience-important. Accessed 7 Apr. 2020.

[3] "Report: Robots Will Replace 20 Million Manufacturing Jobs by ...." 26 Jun. 2019, https://www.usnews.com/news/econ omy/articles/2019-06-26/report-robots-will-replace-20-million-manufacturing-jobs-by-2030. Accessed 7 Apr. 2020.

[4] "Student Loan Debt Statistics In 2020: A Record $1.6 Tril-lion." 3 Feb. 2020, https://www.forbes.com/sites/zackfriedman/ 2020/02/03/student-loan-debt-statistics/. Accessed 7 Apr. 2020.

[5] "Student Loan Resources: Financial Aid & Loan Debt ...." https://www.debt.org/students/. Accessed 7 Apr. 2020.

[6] "U.S. Median Household Income Up in 2018 From 2017." https://www.census.gov/library/stories/2019/09/us-median-

household-income-up-in-2018-from-2017.html. Accessed 7 Apr. 2020.

[7] "Your lifetime earnings are probably determined in your 20s ...." 10 Feb. 2015, https://www.washingtonpost.com/news/wonk/wp/2015/02/10/your-lifetime-earnings-are-probably-determined-in-your-twenties/. Accessed 8 Apr. 2020.

[8] "Maslow's Hierarchy of Needs Explained ...." 24 Feb. 2020, https://www.thoughtco.com/maslows-hierarchy-of-needs-4582571. Accessed 8 Apr. 2020.

[9] "Tax Rates by State - WalletHub." 10 Mar. 2020, https://wallethub.com/edu/best-worst-states-to-be-a-taxpayer/2416/. Accessed 9 Apr. 2020.

[10] "How to Ace the 50 Most Common Job Interview Questions ...." 4 Jun. 2015, https://www.inc.com/travis-bradberry/how-to-ace-the-50-most-common-interview-questions.html. Accessed 13 Apr. 2020.

[11] "ADP BrandVoice: The Costs Of Training New Employees ...." 2 Jun. 2017, https://www.forbes.com/sites/adp/2017/06/02/the-costs-of-training-new-employees-including-hidden-expenses/. Accessed 13 Apr. 2020.

Made in the USA
Columbia, SC
26 July 2023

6815cb4b-6b94-42e6-8c79-33bd2dea58bfR01